Inside "The Lion, the Witch and the Wardrobe"

James Stuart Bell,
Carrie Pyykkonen, and
Linda Washington

ST. MARTIN'S GRIFFIN   NEW YORK

Inside "The Lion, the Witch and the Wardrobe"

MYTHS, MYSTERIES, AND
MAGIC FROM
"THE CHRONICLES OF NARNIA"

www.stmartins.com

Unless otherwise noted, all Scriptures are taken from the Holy Bible, the New American Standard Version © 1960, 1962, 1963, 1968, 1971, 1973, 1975, 1977 by the Lockman Foundation, and the New International Version © 1973, 1978, 1984 by the International Bible Society.

Cover illustration by Cliff Nielsen
Interior illustrations by Jonathan Bennett
Book design by Gretchen Achilles

Library of Congress Cataloging-in-Publication Data

Bell, James S.
 Inside "The Lion, the Witch and the Wardrobe" : myths, mysteries, and magic from the Chronicles of Narnia / James Stuart Bell, Carrie Pyykkonen, and Linda Washington.
  p. cm.
 ISBN 0-312-34744-8
 EAN 978-0-312-34744-4
 1. Lewis, C. S. (Clive Staples), 1898–1963. Chronicles of Narnia—Juvenile literature. 2. Children's stories, English—Appreciation—Juvenile literature. 3. Fantasy fiction, English—Appreciation—Juvenile literature. 4. Narnia (Imaginary place)—Juvenile literature. 5. Magic in literature—Juvenile literature. 6. Myth in literature—Juvenile literature. I. Pyykkonen, Carrie. II. Washington, Linda M. III. Title.

PR6023.E926C53225 2005
823.912—dc22   2005048377

First Edition: November 2005

10   9   8   7   6   5   4   3   2   1

To all the tweeners in our lives . . .
Caitie, Chloe, Jasmine, Joseph, Kelsey, Lamont, Larissa, Samantha,
Samuel, Sarah, Sean, and Tyanna
Our hope for all of you: dream big, be inquisitive, and never
  lose sight of the Aslan of our world. (He will never lose sight
  of you.)

P.S. C. S. Lewis was right—you are never too old for fairy tales.

Contents

Acknowledgments

We had so much fun writing this book! If it weren't for the following people, this book would have lacked proper grammar, coherent themes, and a very snazzy Turkish Delight quiz. What we are trying to say is we are so thankful for the inquisitive, irreplaceable people who kept us in line and in a very strict behavioral program.

Of course, the behavioral program should be credited to Benjamin Pyykkonen. Without Ben, we would still be trying to assemble Linda's wardrobe, two children would have lacked supervision during the writing phase, and the laundry would still be piled up.

Also, thanks are offered to the youth group of Church of the Great Shepherd in Wheaton, Illinois, for participating in the unofficial Turkish Delight survey. Your responses were invaluable and we are very thankful that no one spit out the treats in our sight. (You must've taught them right, Dane!)

To the people who helped research flowers and tested quizzes. Stan and Gia Washington, Larissa Pyykkonen, and Linda Van Dine, thank you for avoiding your work to do ours.

With much gratitude to the staff of Marion E. Wade Center of Wheaton College (Heidi, Sean, and Jake) for their support of our explorations in the C. S. Lewis section. Special thanks to whoever put all the books back after our visits (of course, we would have done it ourselves if we were allowed).

To George Kacena, who happened to show up when we needed him most. Thank you for letting us use you as a reference for entrance into the Wade Center and also suggesting Lyle Dorsett's name (oh, hope you don't mind, Lyle). We are also thankful to Lyle Dorsett for his interest and knowledge of C. S. Lewis, which was inspirational to us all.

Thankful are we also for Wheaton Public Library for their books on topics from tea parties to wolves to moss. We are grateful that our weighty checkouts were not condemned and they still accept our library cards.

Panera Bread in Bloomingdale, Illinois, is worthy of many thanks, too. As we sipped soup and ate cookies, this book took shape while sitting among the aroma of their freshly baked breads.

Thank you to Giles Anderson and Marc Resnick for giving us this opportunity to show off the many fun layers of C. S. Lewis's masterpiece, *The Lion, the Witch and the Wardrobe*.

We are also greatly thankful for the encouragement and support of the following people: Geoff Allen, the Bakers, Marilyn Brenner, the Brummunds, Vicki Cairns, Alice Costabile, John and Danielle Crilly, the Curtises, Donn & Kathleen Czegus, Danilo Diedrichs, Anne Goldsmith, Becky Hanselman, Mark & Becky Nesbitt, Sile ni Chionna, Maralee Parker, Paavo & Darlene Pyykkonen, Andy Saur, Marlise Schiltz, John Schultz, Betty Swanberg, Preston & Susie Washington, Linda Willet, and Colleen Yang.

With utmost respect we thank C. S. Lewis for the childlike heart and brilliant intellect that created an unforgettable story of talking beasts, lovable children, and an untamable lion.

Thank you Lord, Jesus Christ, for being our sacrificial lamb, the Lion of Judah.

Stop Right There!

ey, you—you with the book in your hand. No, don't put it down. There's no turning back now. You might as well keep reading.

You've picked up this book for one reason—well, maybe two:

1. Because your mom/grandpa/cousin It thinks you need to read it, so you're just humoring him/her/it, because he/she/it is staring at you *right now*.

2. You want to know what the big deal is about *The Lion, the Witch and the Wardrobe*. No harm in that. For over fifty years, millions of people have been curious about this very book.

Expert, Intermediate, or Novice?

Since you're going to read this book anyway (might as well, since you've come this far), we'd like to make a quick suggestion. First of all, decide what you are. No, we don't mean the obvious I'm a ten-/eleven-/thirty-seven-year-old boy/girl stuff. We're talking about what you are in regard to how much you know about *The Lion, the Witch and the Wardrobe* (or *LWW*, as we'll call it from now on . . . come on now, say it with feeling, "L-W-W") by Clive Staples Lewis (otherwise known as C. S. Lewis). Are you

- an **Expert**—someone who already knows everything about *LWW* and wants to test your knowledge?

- an **Intermediate**—someone who knows an average amount of information about *LWW*?

- a **Novice**—someone who knows next to nothing about Narnia? Let's face it. Your first question was "Narnia? Who's she?" Admit it.

Regardless of your knowledge of Lewis's book or lack of it, this book can meet your information needs. But we wouldn't want you to waste time reading pages you don't *have* to read. We know how busy you are. To show that we care, we invite you to choose the category below that fits your level of knowledge about *LWW* and read *only* the suggested pages.

- **Expert**—Read all of the WHITE pages in this book

- **Intermediate**—Read all of the WHITE pages in this book

- **Novice**—Read all of the WHITE pages in this book

Know what to read now? Okay—Let's get started! First . . .

𝔄 Little Background

The Lion, the Witch and the Wardrobe (whoops! *LWW*) was published in 1950, probably before your mom or dad was born. (Imagine that!) But the idea for *LWW* began waaaayyy before that, when C. S. Lewis was just a kid in Belfast, Northern Ireland.

Thumb front view Thumb side view

(He was born on November 29, 1898—an even longer time ago!)

Now, take a quick look at your thumb. Go on! Count the joints in it.

You've got two joints, right? (Okay, count 'em again.) Get this: C. S. Lewis had only *one* joint on each thumb. Yes, really! Because he had a hard time building things, he started writing stories. (Every kid's gotta do something.)

Being left alone a lot in a large house in the country outside of Belfast inspired his imagination. (His mother, Flora, died just before he turned ten and Albert, his dad, was busy working.) "Little Lea," the house Lewis's family moved into in 1905, had a big attic and lots of passages and books to explore.

Lewis soon found that he liked to make up stories about "dressed animals." These stories became part of "Animal-Land," an imaginary world he shared with his brother, Warren, who was three years older. Warren (aka Warnie), however, had his own "country"— India, one that bore a passing resemblance to the real one.[1]

When he was a teen, C. S. Lewis—or Jack, as he preferred to be called, because he didn't like his first name (he liked his dog's name instead)—wrote a story called "Boxen: or Scenes from Boxonian City Life."[2] It involved the union of two kingdoms: India and Animal-land. Now, Animal-land wasn't *exactly* like Narnia any more than you're like your aunt Noreen. Lewis wouldn't even begin to develop Narnia until he was forty—long after he began teaching at Oxford University.

[1] Lewis talks all about this in his autobiography, *Surprised by Joy* (London: Geoffrey Bles, 1956. New York: Harcourt, Brace, Jovanovich, 1956). (Like this footnote? There are more just like it in the book. Keep reading!)
[2] Your library might have a copy of *Boxen: The imaginary World of the Young C. S. Lewis,* edited by Walter Hooper (New York: Harcourt Brace Jovanovich, 1985).

What We'll Tell You About C. S. Lewis

We could tell you more about his life, how he stopped believing in God after his mother's death, how he grew up to attend Oxford as a student, taught there, and later taught at Cambridge, the friends (Arthur Greeves, Owen Barfield, J. R. R. Tolkien, and others) he made, how he fought in World War I, how he started believing in God again, and how he married for the first and only time at the age of fifty-seven. Actually, we'll get to some of that later in this book. But really our job is simply to tell you about what led him to write *LWW*. There are plenty of biographies of C. S. Lewis that provide more information about his life.[3]

Throughout his life, C. S. Lewis loved fairy tales and other fantasy stories like *Gulliver's Travels* by Jonathan Swift, the *Iliad* and the *Odyssey* (Homer—and we don't mean Simpson), *Le Morte d'Arthur* by Thomas Malory, as well as children's books by Edith Nesbit (*Five Children and It* and *The Amulet*), George Macdonald (*The Princess and the Goblin*), Beatrix Potter (*The Tale of Peter Rabbit, The Tale of Squirrel Nutkin*), and Kenneth Grahame (*The Wind in the Willows*). (Some books were longer-loved than others.) He also liked books by H. G. Wells (*The Time Machine*). Maybe you've read books by these authors, too. (For more about them, see chapter 5c.)

As you read this book (the book in your hand), you'll find more information about C. S. Lewis's past as well as his deepest beliefs, which caused him to write the story that he did. That story of course is the great adventure story called *The Lion, the Witch and the Wardrobe* (*LWW*).

Come explore with us!

---

[3] For example: *C. S. Lewis: Through the Shadowlands* by Brian Sibley (Grand Rapids, MI: Fleming H.Revell, 1985, 1994) and *Jack: A Life of C. S. Lewis* by George Sayer (Wheaton, IL: Crossway Books).

By the way, you can read this book two ways:

- From cover to cover (We hope you'll do that!)

- By topics. If you choose this option, the table of contents will be your best friend (But we'll be yours if you choose the first option).

Some Freebies You Get with the Purchase of This Book

- Narnia Knowledge (or NK for short): Every so often we'll define a word or phrase from the book or tell you about a fairy-tale creature Lewis mentions (for example, satyrs) that you might've wondered about. Be on the lookout!

- Exciting facts about C. S. Lewis, history, science, and other cool stuffs (wars, wolves, and wardrobes)

- Random quizzes and lists

- 46 Uses for Handkerchiefs and Other "Faun" Things (You never know when these will be useful in your life.)

- An unofficial Turkish Delight survey (We risked life and limb to get you the facts.)

- Ta-Duh Facts. Not ta-da. We mean, ta-duh. These are facts that you may or may not know (for example, who the "real" Lucy was in C. S. Lewis's life; how a road is made; etc.). If you know them, you'll probably just roll your eyes and go, "Duh. I already knew that." See? That's why we call them "Ta-Duh Facts."

- A study guide you can use in your very own Narnia Book Club

CHAPTER ONE

Four Kids and a War(drobe)

Into the Twilight Zone

In 1959–64 (aaaaaaaaages ago), a weekly half-hour TV show called *The Twilight Zone,* created by an innovative (an adjective meaning "capable of making something new") man named Rod Serling, was in production. (Reruns are shown on the SciFi channel and are on DVD.) Wondering what that's got to do with *LWW*? Plenty. Sit tight and you'll find out.

In each *Twilight Zone* episode, various characters would find themselves in strange worlds or in situations extremely different from the reality they were used to (unless they were *used* to being chased by maniacal talking dolls or zombielike neighbors). Whenever they discovered something out of the ordinary, the narrator of the show, Rod Serling, would suddenly pop up and announce that the character had "crossed over into the twilight zone." (This was another strange occurrence. After all, when was the last time a narrator popped up in your living room and began discussing your life?) Then the eerie theme music would play (*Doo doo doo doo, doo doo doo doo*).

If you've read *LWW,* you know that a girl named Lucy Pevensie was the first person in her family to cross over into a "twilight zone" known as Narnia. (Check out "All About Lucy" at the end of the chapter.) How did she get there? Through a wardrobe.

(Give yourself minus 50 points if you said an airplane or any other form of transportation.)

Imagine opening your closet door and discovering a completely different world beyond *your* clothes. (Have you checked what's beyond your closet lately? Go on. Give it a try. We dare you.)

If you're back from checking out your closet, let's get back to the fictional Lucy. We first meet Lucy and her siblings Peter, Susan, and Edmund as they arrive at the country home of Professor Kirke (a man curiously like C. S. Lewis) during World War II, having traveled all the way from London.

Lucy, Peter, Susan, and Edmund didn't have much choice about living with the Professor. They *had* to live there. Imagine having to live with total strangers—strangers who were told they *had* to take you in. How would you feel? This is the situation Lucy and her siblings found themselves in. Little did they know that the Professor's home would be the key to some of the greatest adventures of their lives! It all began when they decided to explore the many rooms of the Professor's country house. (For exploration ideas or tips on what to do for a rainy day, see the games at the end of the chapter.) That's when Lucy discovered the wardrobe in a spare room. (Wondering what a wardrobe is? Look for "And Now, a Word About Wardrobes" later in the chapter. No need to thank us.)

Early Inspirations

Another girl went through a wardrobe in a spare room and found herself in a strange place. Her name was Amabel (that's right—Amabel, not Anabel or Annabelle) and she's the main character in "The Aunt and Amabel," one of the short stories in *The Magic World* by E. Nesbit (published in 1912). (For more on E. Nesbit, see chapter 5c.)

If you haven't read "The Aunt and Amabel," maybe you won't mind us telling you some of the plot. Eight-year-old Amabel performs an act she believes is thoughtful, but her aunt thinks otherwise. Result: punishment for Amabel. She winds up spending the day in a room with a large wardrobe. But that room is the site of a huge adventure, which begins with the discovery of a train timetable. On it she sees a curious station name: *Bigwardrobeinspareroom*. After climbing into the wardrobe, she winds up at a curious place called *Whereyouwantogoto*.

Although C. S. Lewis read this story years before writing *LWW*, it's doubtful that he had it in mind while writing his book.

Operation Evacuation

Like the Pevensies, many kids in real life (about 2 million) were sent out of London before and after German forces bombed the city during World War II. This attack was known as the Blitz and was part of a planned invasion of Britain by Nazi forces ("Operation Sea Lion"). Pretty soon, there was a full-scale air battle called the Battle of Britain.

Check out this handy time line of some of the events of WWII:

WORLD WAR II TIME LINE

September 1, 1939
Invasion of Poland by the Nazis

September 3, 1939
Britain joins France, New Zealand, and Australia in declaring war on Germany. Parents begin sending their children out of London.

January 8, 1940
The British begin rationing.

July 10, 1940
The beginning of the Battle of Britain

August 15, 1940
Air raids over Britain begin.

The bombing of London began in 1940 and continued through 1941. Imagine how scared the people of London were during that time. (If you happened to live in New York during the attacks on the World Trade Center in 2001, you have some idea of how scary and horrible a time it was.)

With the constant threat of air raids (attacks by enemy aircrafts), many parents knew that their kids wouldn't be safe in the city. So, they sent them away by train to live with families in the country. If you lived in London during this time, your mom or dad might have done the same thing.

The evacuations began in September 1939, just as the German forces invaded Poland. Signs were posted all over London, alerting people as to when and where the evacuations would take place.

Many kids were evacuated through their schools. Most traveled light, bringing only a gas mask, a toothbrush, an ID card, and a change of underwear. (Since the gas masks were red and blue, they were called "Mickey Mouse" masks. Wanna guess why?)

After arriving at a town or village station, the kids would be divided among the families in the area, who were under orders to provide homes for them. (When a person is under orders to report to a place, you would say that he or she is *billeted* to that location. Amaze your friends with your keen vocabulary.)

ᚼis ᚼome Was Their ᚼome

Even C. S. Lewis had wartime guests, probably starting in September 1939.[1] His home had enough room for four kids. A group of girls from London stayed at his country home on the outskirts of Oxford. They didn't all arrive at once. They were sent to his home in stages. Some of the girls stayed for more than a year.

While two of the girls (Patricia Boshell and Marie Bosc) arrived, Lewis was busy in the garden. Since he wore dirty gardening clothes, one of them assumed he was the gardener! At least he could laugh about it.

At this point, Lewis taught at Oxford University and shared a home ("the Kilns") with his brother, Warren, and Janie and

[1] We found conflicting information on this fact. In the book of his letters, *C. S. Lewis Collected Letters: Books, Broadcasts and War 1931–1949* Vol. 2, ed. Walter Hooper (New York: Harper Collins, 2004), some letters dated 1939 mentioned the arrival of the girls to Lewis's home. But another book listed their arrival starting in 1940.

Maureen Moore—the mother and sister of his friend Paddy, who had been killed during World War I (more on that in chapter 16). Mrs. Moore (whose nickname was Minto, but not like Mentos the mints) lived there until she was placed in a nursing home in 1950.

Because of the air raids (or threat of them), blackouts took place, even in the country. Everyone was told to hang black fabric against the windows each night. With everything dark, Nazi bombers would have a harder time finding targets.

Keep in mind that food, gas, clothes, and coal were rationed then. Officials feared that food supplies would run out, so everyone was allotted a certain amount of food (a *ration*). Ration books were handed out so that everyone could keep track of food items like eggs, butter, and sugar. Even kids had ration books. Perhaps the Pevensies brought theirs to the Professor's house. C. S. Lewis's boarders would have each had one. (Try to imagine what rationing would be like now. How would you feel if a limit was placed on the amount of food you could eat each week?)

At this point in his life, Lewis had little experience with kids. Although he thought his guests were nice and all (as he told his brother in a letter), their presence was a challenge for a busy professor, especially since they kept asking for advice on what to do.[2] (Maybe that's why he made the Pevensies able to entertain themselves at the Professor's house. They're like you in that regard, right?) Still, he liked having them around.

His wartime boarders gave him good material for a story. At first, he thought about writing a story about four kids (Rose, Peter, Martin, and Ann) who were sent to the home of an old professor. (Sounds familiar.) But the land of Narnia you know and love was still to be developed. (More on that in chapter 5b. You

---

[2] Hello again from footnote land. Anyway, many of C. S. Lewis's biographies go into more depth about Lewis, the Moores, and Warren. Pick up one or two at your local library. We mentioned a couple in the footnotes in the Introduction.

can wait that long, right? Unless you want to skip ahead and read it right now. We won't tell.)

But it all started with a wardrobe.

𝕬nd 𝕹ow, a 𝕎ord 𝕬bout 𝕎ardrobes

Some rooms in old houses like Professor Kirke's didn't have closets. Wardrobes—big, wooden cabinets really—were used for storing clothes.

C. S. Lewis may have been inspired to write about a wardrobe by one that his grandfather made (pictured below), which occupied a space in his childhood home, Little Lea, back in Belfast. The wardrobe (Lucy Pevensie not included) currently resides at Marion E. Wade Center in Wheaton, Illinois.

Used by permission of Marion E. Wade Center, Wheaton College, Wheaton, IL.

Another source of inspiration for *LWW* came from one of the girls evacuated from London who asked Lewis what was in an old wardrobe. Could she explore it? Her question undoubtedly stayed in Lewis's mind (kind of like a song that just won't leave your head).

In chapter 1 of *LWW*, Lucy did just what Lewis's wartime boarder did—she explored a wardrobe. There she discovered more than just a bunch of old fur coats and other clothes. Like Dorothy in *The Wonderful Wizard of*

Oz, she found a new world to explore—a world quite different from the one she just left. This was Narnia.

The first creature she met in Narnia was a faun: Mr. Tumnus. (You don't see fauns every day . . . or ever!) Meeting Mr. Tumnus sets up the *conflict* (the central problem) of the story. In chapter 2 of this book, you'll read more about fauns and handkerchiefs than you probably ever thought you would.

Rainy-Day Games

Being stuck inside on a rainy day during summer vacation can be quite a bummer if you haven't a clue what to do. It's especially hard to stay indoors when you have your heart set on such splendid activities as riding bikes or playing with friends.

Peter, Susan, Edmund, and Lucy found themselves in a similar situation. The children had their hearts set on exploring the grounds and neighboring woods and mountains, but instead found themselves indoors.

Rain can sometimes be quite a bothersome thing, but as in almost all situations that seem disappointing, there is the opportunity for something good to happen—even adventure. It took time for the Pevensie children to warm up to the idea of having fun indoors, but of course having a good time is a choice. Peter, Susan, Edmund, and Lucy were ready to make something good happen even during a dreary day.

Sometimes adventure finds us in the most unlikely places. Adventure found Lucy through what looked like a plain old wardrobe. She became the first in her family to enter Narnia.

Even if you have lived in the same place for years, you may want to take a closer look at your surroundings. Have you noticed everything? There probably is something new and exciting to discover. Are you stuck indoors today? If so, try exploring or do one of the other rainy-day activities listed below.

IDEAS FROM THE PEVENSIES

- **Read a book.** Susan suggests reading books for entertainment while it is raining outside. Why not read one of the Narnia books or another favorite book of your choice?

- **Exploring.** Lucy discovers Narnia during an exploration of the Professor's house. What will you find in your house?

OTHER IDEAS

- **Story writing.** Write a story and draw your own illustrations about what you would hope to find if you entered a wardrobe.

- **Scavenger hunt.** Create a list of items using *LWW* as a guide. Split up into teams and see how many items you can find on the list. For instance, try to find an umbrella, a Bible, and a wireless (a radio).

- **House building.** Create a model of the Professor's house using household items such as cereal boxes and cans, don't forget about having many doors. When you're finished, try to imagine what would be behind each door.

All About Lucy

AGE: Eight or nine

BIRTH ORDER: She's the youngest Pevensie.

NICKNAME(S): Lu

QUALITIES: She's honest, loyal, helpful, perceptive, and fearful. Yet she's also adventurous. After all, she didn't back out of the wardrobe after finding out that it led to a different world. She also didn't say no to visiting a strange faun at his house (chapter 2). And she later insisted that her brothers and sister help the faun after learning of his arrest. Also, she was the only one besides Susan to follow Aslan when he surrendered himself to the witch (see chapters 14 and 15).

CLAIM TO FAME: She was the first to enter Narnia and the one who encouraged her siblings to help Mr. Tumnus.

LIKES/LOVES: Exploring old houses; the smell and feel of fur; the faun Mr. Tumnus; being truthful

DISLIKES: Being called a liar

GIFT FROM FATHER CHRISTMAS: A vial with a cordial; a dagger

NARNIA TITLE(S): Queen Lucy; Lucy the Valiant; Daughter of Eve

CHAPTER TWO

Why the Egg Was Brown and Other Questions You May or May Not Care About!

Inquisitiveness

Have you ever wondered why the earth is round or why skittles come in different colors? We have. This is what is called inquisitiveness, just trying to figure things out or simply being curious. Lucy's inquisitiveness was the fuel that drove her feet past the fur coats right into the land of Narnia. Learning new things can be fun! *LWW* ignites the inquisitive mind to ask all kinds of questions that deserve exploration. Let's continue on as inquisitive readers and learn some interesting facts that are worthy of consideration.

WHY IS THE EGG BROWN?

We are so glad you asked! Of course the more important question is which came first, the chicken or the egg? Scientists believe that it is actually the . . . *just kidding*. We are not going to get into this ongoing and never-ending debate (ask your parents).

However, we do know that the color of an egg has to do with the breed of the hen that lays the egg. A brown (also known as red) hen lays brown eggs and a white hen lays white eggs. That was pretty simple. Did you know that there are no significant nutritional differences between white and brown eggs? So, eat the one you like best! Apparently Mr. Tumnus prefers the brown variety, or are there only brown chickens in Narnia? What do you think?

IS A STRANGE FAUN STRANGER IF IT IS A STRANGER?

Perhaps it is strange to meet a faun in a foreign land, but probably even rarer to meet one in your own land. Lucy's first faun meeting was soon after she pushed through those furs in the wardrobe. Do you think it would be strange to meet a being that is half goat and half human? We thought meeting a faun would score a strange rating of three: Strange because it is an unfamiliar creature; strange because fauns are just strange by nature; and strange because he/she/it is a stranger.

The faun Lucy met was, of course, readers, Mr. Tumnus. Mr. Tumnus definitely showed signs of being strange—such as his nervous chatter, his very tidy cave home, and what's with the umbrella! But we should be quick to point out that as Mr. Tumnus became less of a stranger, he became less strange. And of all the things Mr. Tumnus is, he is inquisitive, just like you, reader.

WHAT DO WE KNOW ABOUT MR. TUMNUS?

By exploring Mr. Tumnus's living quarters we can get a peek at what kind of faun he really is. The faun in question lived in a cave. Caves are typically good for exploring but a little too dark, dreary, and cold to reside in. Would you want to live in a cave? As bizarre as a home in a cave is to us, Narnia definitely is bound to have its differences to England, and America, so perhaps living in a cave is not so strange to a Narnian. Lucy must have felt a little awkward going into a stranger's cave. But imagine talking to a faun in the land of Narnia, which is definitely a strange experience. However, inside the faun's house many things were familiar to Lucy. After all, Mr. Tumnus had books, a kettle for tea, a table and chairs to sit on. We, lovers of stories and books, found Mr. Tumnus's library quite interesting.

BOOKS WE KNOW ARE IN MR. TUMNUS'S LIBRARY . . .

The Life and Letters of Silenus or Nymphs and Their Ways

Men, Monks, and Gamekeepers; A Study in Popular Legend

Is Man a Myth?

BOOKS WE THOUGHT WOULD BE IN MR. TUMNUS'S LIBRARY . . .

How to Kidnap Without Guilt

The History of Narnian Winters

Why Christmas Became Extinct

Books you think would be in Mr. Tumnus's library (go ahead, give it a try) . . .

_____

_____

_____

All About Mr. Tumnus

AGE: Middle-aged during the rule of Peter, Susan, Edmund, and Lucy

UNUSUAL CHARACTERISTICS: Strange verse (talk); obsessive umbrella use

NICKNAME(S): Unknown ("Tums" might be nice, though)

QUALITIES: Good housekeeper; kind

CLAIM TO FAME: First named and honored by the enthroned children

LIKES/LOVES: Aslan, tea, books, the flute

DISLIKES: The White Witch; it being always winter and never Christmas

IS KIDNAPPING REALLY THE ANSWER?

We hate to bring up the unfortunate truth about Mr. Tumnus's employment. It really is a shame that Mr. Tumnus ever had contact with the White Witch at all. It is clear that Mr. Tumnus was scared of what the witch would do to him if he did not comply with her wishes. So Mr. Tumnus with a guilty heart told the witch that if he met a human he would kidnap him or her and take them straight to her.

Do you know how it feels when we do something wrong but we are to scared to do what is right? As time goes on, we start feeling guilty. Then, because guilt feels so awful, we try to hide that hurt and try to forget we ever did wrong. Well, Mr. Tumnus wanted to pretend that he wasn't doing wrong. He had convinced himself that humans were somewhat lower than he was, so perhaps it was all right to trick them and give them over to the White Witch. But then he actually met a Daughter of Eve and it was clear that she was very pleasant indeed. We are, of course, talking about Lucy, someone with many good qualities. The faun had two options: he could continue with his plan of kidnapping or repent of his ways.

Confessing your wrongs is a very difficult thing to do. There are many ways to say sorry and ask for forgiveness. Mr. Tumnus is one of those fauns who apparently makes a puddle on the floor with his tears. No matter how you go about admitting your misdeeds, the important thing is your heart. It is clear in the story of Mr. Tumnus that he was truly sorry for what he did. Because of this ability to be truthful, a beautiful friendship developed between Lucy and Mr. Tumnus.

Lucy, a good friend, shows care for Mr. Tumnus throughout their time with each other. One way she shows kindness is by giving him a handkerchief to catch his tears. You might think that handkerchiefs only have one use and therefore are not very good gifts, but we came up with forty-five uses for them. Oh, and uses for one other "fun" or "faun" thing.

46 USES FOR HANDKERCHIEFS AND OTHER "FAUN" THINGS

Disclaimer #1: Do *not* steal all those unused, still-in-the-box hankies that you gave to your dad the last five Christmases

Disclaimer #2: We are not in any way shape or form professional handkerchief and other "faun" things experts. Proceed with caution . . .

Disclaimer #3: "Faun" things are best used when clean and dry, unlike the handkerchief that Lucy provided for Mr. Tumnus's use

1. Practice napkin folding

2. Make an airplane

3. Use to cut out a snowflake ornament to hang on the Christmas tree

4. Doll hammock

5. Beauty-sleep eye mask

6. Bandanna to use on your head

7. A square on a quilt

8. Kite

9. Tablecloth for a table in a dollhouse

10. Object of tug-a-war

11. A doily

12. Mummy wrap

13. Old-style slingshot

14. Pick up hot things

15. Polish furniture

16. Wipe sweat

17. Parachute for G.I. Joe

18. Blow nose

19. Flag in the game Capture the Flag

20. Entertain yourself by waving side to side

21. Surrender in a war

22. Magic tricks

23. Picnic blanket for Barbie

24. Guinea pig ghost costume

25. Kitty blanket

26. Pillowcase for a rabbit pillow

27. Very soft origami

28. Doll sheet

29. Ponytail holder

30. Sling for an injured doll arm

31. Doll shawl

32. Scarf for a cold bird

33. Mask to keep secret identity safe

34. Sail for small sailboat

35. Wall decoration

36. Big pocket for clown costume

37. Hamster hammock

38. Wedding dress or veil for doll

39. Napkin

40. Bread warmer

41. Diaper

42. Tent for Action Figure

43. Fill with catnip for a cat toy

44. Capture frogs

45. A sack to carry things

46. Umbrella (the other faun thing)—use it for rain, silly!
    Okay, so in some places people use them to keep sun out
    of their face. Maybe even some people use umbrellas to
    protect themselves from snow like Mr. Tumnus, but you
    already know he is strange

TA-DUH!

Inquisitiveness Revisited

Reader, you will actually see the word *inquisitive* later on in the
story of *LWW*. C. S. Lewis uses this word in chapter 2 to question
why Edmund did not notice that a character was being inquisitive. Which is always a valid question to ask if someone is trying
to learn a lot about you but does not tell you very much about
him- or herself. Inquisitiveness is such a wonderful thing but can
be used wrongly, as you will find out later. So, inquisitive minds
please continue on your quest to learn and explore with the
heart of Lucy and not the scheming of the White Witch.

WHY IS LUCY CALLED A DAUGHTER OF EVE?

If you do meet a faun, please remember it may be confused about
what you are. You may be asked if you are a Daughter of Eve or a
Son of Adam. It is important to know the proper way to answer
such questions. These phrases about Adam and Eve are another
way to say you are human. C. S. Lewis used these terms in *LWW*

because of his belief in Adam and Eve of the Bible. The Bible refers to Adam and Eve as the first humans God created on earth. Lewis's beliefs were extremely important in how he formed his imaginary land of Narnia. Adam and Eve are part of the Creation story in the Bible. This influenced Lewis to write a Creation story for Narnia. How Narnia came into existence is explained in Lewis's book *The Magician's Nephew*. (Check it out.)

CHAPTER THREE

Don't Get "Carrie-d" Away by a Sleigh

Good Advice

We know what you're thinking. The chapter title is just a clever (okay, clever in our opinion) way of sneaking an author's name into this chapter. No. We're actually performing a vital public service. We're here to point out some important advice you might have missed when you read *LWW*.

But first, a question for you: Are you a fan of suspense or horror films? Maybe while watching one at the theater or on TV (unless you're hiding under a blanket), you've heard some people yelling advice to the characters in the films. Maybe they've said things like, "Hey, don't go in that room! The evil, psychotic gopher just ran in there!" or, "Hey, don't turn your back on that guy! He's got a cream pie in his hand and looks like he wants to use it on you!"

Why do people yell advice to fictional characters (especially since they can't control what the character does or change the action in any way)? As humans, we can't help giving each other advice, especially when we get the impression that a character will run into danger if he or she continues on the path chosen. (Usually, the footprints of the villain leading straight into the wood-shed or to the room with only one exit are a dead giveaway.)

Even though you're not a fictional character, you've probably had advice yelled at you from time to time. Perhaps your parents have just unreeled a string of advice (or commands) for you, beyond the "Choose friends wisely"/"Cover your mouth when you sneeze"/"Don't talk to strangers, especially on the Internet/" "Don't pick on your sister . . . or your nose" variety. Or maybe an older sibling (which could include a twin born a minute sooner than you) feels called upon to give out advice ("If you know what's good for you, you won't touch my stuff ever again!").

Even we have given you advice from time to time. (See the Introduction. See? More advice.)

Teachers are usually good for giving advice (or commands). As a professor and an author, C. S. Lewis often gave advice to the people he taught and to the people who wrote to him. Many kids wrote to him over the years, asking for advice about writing, God, or which books in the Narnia series they should read first. (His answer: whichever one you want. But chronologically, *The Magician's Nephew* comes first, even though it was written after *LWW*.)

As we read chapter 3 in *LWW*, we couldn't help thinking of advice for Lucy and Edmund. C. S. Lewis had some advice for them as well. Check it out:

ADVICE FOR LUCY

- *Never shut yourself up in a wardrobe.* Since C. S. Lewis mentions this not only in chapter 3 (where Lucy follows this advice), but also in chapter 5 (when Peter wisely avoids shutting the wardrobe door completely while inside), we felt this was good advice to bring up. Why is this good advice? Well, wood sometimes expands due to humidity. On a particularly humid day, a door might stick. (Wood also shrinks, but usually not to the size of, say, a door in

Lewis Carroll's *Alice in Wonderland*.) Or, sometimes doorknobs fail to work properly. This happened to the cousin of one of the authors who happened to walk into and shut a closet door that decided not to open when he wanted to leave. The doorknob had to be taken off. All learned a valuable lesson.

- *The best way to win at hide-and-seek is to hide in a totally different country from the one in which people are seeking you.* Obviously, Lucy followed this advice to great advantage. While Peter, Susan, and Edmund looked for her in merrie old England, she went skipping happily off to Narnia. With a strategy like this, she was guaranteed a spot in the Hide-and-Seekers Hall of Fame (if one exists). However, there was another bit of advice she didn't take into consideration.

- *Don't forget that time in Narnia is not the same as time on Earth.* Sadly, Lucy didn't realize the time difference and was not believed when she returned to the Professor's house the first time after spending hours in Narnia. From Peter, Susan, and Edmund's perspective, only moments had passed.

What advice do you have for Lucy? How would your advice add to or change the plot of *LWW*?

ADVICE FOR EDMUND

- *Don't get "Carrie-d" away by a sleigh* (we would have used the word *sledge,* but it doesn't rhyme with *away*). Here's another bit of advice that goes along with that: When approached by a strange woman with a stern face driving a sledge, your best bet is to back away slowly. Of course, that's easy for us to say. We know the whole story.

Unfortunately, Edmund followed our advice only partially, which led to trouble for himself, his siblings, and later Aslan. His decision, we have to admit, made *LWW* a good story. So, we can forgive him for not following our advice. If you read the rest of the story, after believing the lies of the White Witch, he wound up in that very sledge in a later chapter and felt perfectly miserable. See, that's what happens when people fail to listen to our advice.

- *Never openly mock someone about a mythical country you might enter someday*. Once again, Edmund didn't listen to our shouted advice and instead tormented Lucy when she returned from Narnia. He also didn't know anything about foreshadowing in fiction. What's *foreshadowing*? When an author includes a hint that something could happen later in the story, he or she is using a technique known as foreshadowing. The more Edmund mocked Lucy about Narnia, the more certain you are that he will someday enter that country. And what do you know? He did!

- *Never address a queen—even one who didn't acquire the title rightfully—in a rude way.* The White Witch scolded Edmund for his less-than-respectful greeting. Even dictators and those who wrongfully try to attain power know the right way to address a ruler. Since you asked nicely, of course we'll tell you the right way to address a queen. This knowledge may come in handy someday.

There is a certain protocol or "code of conduct" when talking to people in authority.[1] When Edmund took the hint and addressed the White Witch as "Your Majesty," he was using proper etiquette. A queen is usually referred to as "Your Majesty" or "Ma'am." But what if the person you're addressing is a princess rather than a queen? Glad you asked. If you were addressing a princess, you would use the title "Your Royal Highness." (If you saw *Princess Diaries 1* or *2*, you know Mia Thermopolis was addressed that way.)

Knights—what Peter became in chapter 12 of *LWW*—are addressed as "Sir So and So": "Sir Peter," "Sir Belvedere," "Sir Tyrice."

We actually know someone whose wife's aunt is a "lady." Before you can call us ignorant and proclaim that all women are "ladies," keep in mind that "Lady" is a title used for the wife of a knight.

- *Beware eating or drinking anything offered by a stranger who may turn out to be evil*. Edmund obviously failed to take this advice, based on what happened in chapter 4 of *LWW*. Although Lucy didn't take this advice either, judging by her tea party with Mr. Tumnus in chapter 2, at least Mr. Tumnus wasn't evil. (He *considered* kidnapping her, however, as we talked about in chapter 2. Feel free to revisit those pages.)

We can't help thinking about Adam and Eve's temptation to eat the fruit, a story in the Bible. (You can find it in Genesis, chapter 3. Adam and Eve pop up in chapters 2 and 13 of this

---

[1] We found a Web site called I-uk.com, which describes rules of protocol (proper etiquette). It is http://www.i-uk.com/servlet/Front?pagename=OpenMarket/Xcelerate/ShowPage&c=Page&cid=1079976719116 (see—we don't make this stuff up). Interested in looking at it? You may want to check with your parents before checking out any Internet sites. Just a little friendly advice!

British School Uniforms

As we mentioned in chapter 1, many kids were evacuated from London schools. Maybe that's why Edmund and Peter look like they're wearing school uniforms. Evacuated kids weren't allowed to bring a bunch of clothes and other things with them to their temporary homes.

British school uniforms back in the war era and even for some years before that usually consisted of gray knee-length shorts for elementary school boys, a shirt, tie, a sweater, kneesocks, and a blazer. These uniforms set the trend for school uniforms around the world. The colors of the ties varied from school to school.

book. Yes, we know you haven't arrived at chapter 13. We're just giving you something to look forward to.) They took the advice of a snake that turned out to be evil. Look what happened to them.

- *Before taking a stroll in a wintry country, you might want to dress properly.* In all of the illustrations of the Narnia series, we see Edmund in shorts taking a stroll through the snow. The dwarf and the witch on the other hand have fur clothing and are warm and toasty. Oh well. If he's not bothered by the cold, then we're not bothered by it on his behalf. But this wouldn't be a chapter on advice if we didn't bring up the dangers of hypothermia. What's hypothermia? "Subnormal temperature of the body," according to the *Encyclopaedia Britannica.* This is caused by overexposure in cold environments (like, say, walking through a snow-covered country wearing only a school uniform). Hypothermia can be hazardous to one's health. The treatment is to slowly warm up the victim. (Incidentally, the drink the witch gave Edmund in chapter 3 warmed him to a degree. But keep in mind the advice directly above this one.)

What advice do you have for Edmund? How would your advice add to or change the plot of *LWW*?

Ƀow Lucy aŋd Edmuŋd Raŋҟ at Taҟiŋg Advice

Now, let's rank the characters to see how well or how poorly they followed our advice:

GOOD AT TAKING ADVICE							AWFUL AT TAKING ADVICE		
10	9	8	7	6	5	4	3	2	1
		▲ LUCY					▲ EDMUND		

As you can see, Lucy comes up the winner. Edmund, however, could stand to listen to us more often. Let's thank our contestants for playing, shall we?

PAX

When Edmund yelled the word *pax* to Lucy in chapter 3 of *LWW,* did you wonder what it meant? It is a Latin word meaning "peace" and refers to the *Pax Romana,* a time of peace

---

throughout the Mediterranean world. This peace took place between the empires of Augustus Caesar and Marcus Aurelius in the years 27 B.C. to A.D. 180. Wondering who they were? Roman emperors. Augustus Caesar was the emperor around the time of the birth of Christ.

Advice About Reindeer

Since this is a chapter about advice, we thought we'd provide some on reindeer. (Well, our advice is more like *information* about them.) If you happen to find one in your backyard or in the woods near your house (as did the heroine of the movie *Prancer*), this information might prove helpful.

As you know, reindeer pulled the witch's sledge (poor them), just as they power Santa's sleigh (a better job). Obviously, reindeer know how to survive in really cold climates. They have thick fur, for one thing. For another, their hooves allow them good traction in the snow. They stick to eating lichen (a type of fungus) in the winter (and do their own shopping for it by searching for it under the snow) and migrate south by the thousands.

Now, you might wonder how you tell the difference between a reindeer and a caribou. Actually, many believe that, although they look a little different, they might be the same type of animal.

As you know, a reindeer is a larger kind of deer. Those herded and raised by people are smaller (about the size of a donkey) than the ones in the wild. But did you know that both males and female reindeers grow antlers? Yep. They do.

You might have seen reindeer at a Christmas theme park or at a petting zoo at some point. But suppose you wanted to find some out in the wild. Where would you go? We'll tell you: get yourself a plane ticket and head north. You can find some in the forests of Canada (these might be caribou, however), in Alaska, or out on the Arctic tundra (between the North Pole and the timberlines of North America). Or, if you have a lot of time on your hands, head to Siberia or Scandinavia.

The best people to give advice about reindeer are the Sami and the Nenets. Some of the Sami (mountain-dwelling people native to Lapland, Norway, and Finland; they're also called Lapps), and the Nenets (people native to the tundra and forests in northwestern Russia) still herd reindeer as their people have for centuries, but they're not dependent on reindeer to survive.

The Sami and the Nenets use reindeer for transportation (they harness the reindeer to sledges). To herd the reindeer, they use herding dogs.

Advice as Close as Your Daily Newspaper

Speaking of advice, we couldn't close this chapter without a word about advice you can find almost daily. Ever read a newspaper advice column? Two of the most popular syndicated advice columns of all time are "Ask Ann Landers" and "Dear Abby." (About 90 million people read "Ask Ann Landers," by the way.) But did you know that twin sisters wrote these columns? Esther Pauline Friedman, who died in 2002, wrote the "Ann Landers" column, while her sister Pauline wrote under the pen name of Abigail Van Buren ("Dear Abby"). (Pauline's daughter Jeanne now writes the "Dear Abby" column.)

Even though Esther took over the "Ann Landers" column for the *Chicago Sun-Times* in 1955 (it was previously written by a nurse named Ann Landers), "Ask Ann Landers" wasn't the first such column. A journalist named Elizabeth Gilmer (1870–1951) wrote the first advice column back in the 1890s for the *Times-Picayune,* a New Orleans newspaper. Like Esther and Pauline, she wrote under a pen name—Dorothy Dix.

CHAPTER FOUR

Turkish Delight Fit for a Queen

Fit for a Queen

Who has not dreamed of living the life of a royal? What is so intriguing about being a ruler? Perhaps, we just want to be someone we are not. Or, do we long for the power that nobility seems to have? "Servant, bring me some more Turkish Delight," or "Knights, knock down that building so I can have a swimming pool there." Could it be the beautiful wardrobe princes and princesses possess, or having people dote on them, or their apparent happiness? Whatever it is, the truth is, it is very uncommon to experience the life of a princess or prince/king or queen.

Great Britain has a peerage—a way of ordering nobility by using titles. In order the titles used in England are: Duke/Duchess, Marquis/Marchioness, Earl/Countess, Viscount/Viscountess, and Baron/Baroness. Of course, the King and Queen are at the top of the ranks. In England, you have one King and/or Queen. Then you have Princes and Princesses. In Narnia, there are also Kings and Queens who rule the land. In *LWW*, the White Witch calls herself Queen but those loyal to Aslan know he is the true King. Do you know whom Aslan will pick at the end of the story to help rule Narnia?

We learned from the White Witch that not all rulers are good. Even good rulers do not always make good choices. It is a huge responsibility to take care of a whole kingdom. It is pretty easy to label the White Witch; she is just plain mean. Making it always winter and never Christmas is just one of the many ways the White Witch ruled badly.

Quest to Rule Quiz

What type of ruler would you be? Answer the following questions to find out if you are fit to be King or Queen . . .

1. Your kingdom is low on food resources and your people are complaining of hunger. Do you:
   A. Pass out Turkish Delight to all the commoners?
   B. Set up a meeting with your royal council and come up with a long-term plan to diminish hunger?
   C. Tell your people that they are wimps and let them go hungry until they can solve their own problems?

2. Two beavers have fallen into a pit. You are walking by and see the animals stuck in the hole and they are yelling for help. Do you:
   A. Throw a rope into the hole and hoist them out yourself?
   B. Tell the beavers you will send help and have a couple of your servants go back and rescue them from the pit?
   C. Walk by and pretend you do not see or hear them because surely someone else will help them out sooner or later?

3. Harvesters in your kingdom are attempting to get their crops in. They do not have enough workers to get everything done before the crops spoil. Do you:
   A. Send one of your servants to help the harvesters with manual labor?

B. Roll up your royal sleeves and help get the crop harvested?

C. Demand part of harvest as payment for your awesome-ness as ruler of the land?

4. A poor peasant is caught stealing a loaf of bread from a local vendor. The authorities bring the thief to you for consequences for their only attempt ever at stealing. The peasant promises to never steal again. Do you:

   A. Cut off their head?

   B. Have them work 80 hours of community service for the vendor that they stole from with no payment?

   C. Put them in jail for five years?

5. Your father is determined that you start acting like the royal you are and asks you in some way of your choice to refine yourself. Do you:

   A. Take extra fencing lessons to show your father that you are tough and disciplined?

   B. Ignore your dad's request with the realization that you will rule the kingdom someday anyway?

   C. Read up on your kingdom's history to ensure that you will not repeat bad decisions made by some of your ancestors?

6. Your family is hosting a royal ball. Your mother, the Queen, has put you in charge of the guest list. Do you:

   A. Invite the whole kingdom?

   B. Invite only those people who can pay a $50 fee?

   C. Forget the invitations, people will still come anyway, right?

7. Your royal pain of a sister has been running around the castle tormenting the household help. An hour ago you witnessed

her put a pound of salt in the cook's soup when he had his back turned. Do you:

A. Tell her you will tell on her if she does not give you her brand-new kite?
B. Confront her and ask her to confess to the cook and your parents herself. If she does not comply, go tell your parents and the cook before she serves the salty soup?
C. Go tell your parents what she did and let them deal with her?

8. The gate to one of the castle's horse pens is mistakenly left open. Your favorite horse, Drobe, gets out and cannot be found. Do you:
A. Decide it is not a big deal because you have so many other horses?
B. Send all the kingdom's finest riders to go look for your horse?
C. Put up flyers around the kingdom that inform the people that Drobe is missing and give a $200 dollar reward to whoever finds him?

9. You have two obligations for this evening. One is an important meeting with the your advisers concerning a deadly plague that hit the neighboring kingdom to the west. The other is a birthday party for your school friend, Joy. Do you:
A. Spend half your evening at the party and then show up late for the meeting?
B. Skip the party and attend the important meeting with your advisers?
C. Forget the meeting and go party for the whole evening; after all, you are only young once?

10. Your kingdom is divided in thought. Half of the kingdom

wants a fountain installed in front of the castle and the
other half wants a statue of Mr. Tumnus. Do you:

A. Put it to a vote?

B. Do both (a Mr. Tumnus Fountain)?

C. Put up a statue of yourself?

(See end of chapter for scoring.)

ASLAN'S CHOSEN (25–30 POINTS)

You are fit to be a king or queen by Aslan's standards. You are generous and kind and you look at the whole picture.

PRINCE/PRINCESS FOREVER (15–24)

You have a good heart and good intentions. You are in the process of learning how to make choices that take your people's needs and desires into consideration.

A ROYAL PAIN (0–14)

You are not the White Witch but are starting to walk down the same path she did. Give yourself another chance to make good choices as a ruler of Narnia and take the quiz again. This second chance is called "grace" and it is yours freely.

Turkish Delight

Just Imagine that a witch finds you in the middle of the forest. You have a feeling that she is a suspicious character: at least you notice her stern face and she has called you an idiot. The witch offers you a warm drink in the midst of the bitterness of the winter day. Without even thinking, you take the drink and consume it. Now she is telling you that you can have any food your heart desires. The drink, by the way, was pretty tasty. Edmund knew right away what to ask for: Turkish Delight. What would you have wanted? Is there a food you cannot resist, perhaps ice cream or a favorite candy? Would you have accepted the witch's offer!

We were wondering why Edmund could not resist Turkish Delight. What is so special about this confection? A confection is a sweet treat or candy. Turkish Delight is one of the oldest confections in the world. Many enjoy this treat with a hot liquid such as coffee. Do you think the drink Edmund got from the witch was coffee? We have even heard that some people eat the sweet to freshen their breath. Well, Edmund at least didn't have bad breath during his adventures in Narnia.

The sweet that Lewis called Turkish Delight was originally called *Lokum* and is still called that today in the Eastern part of the world. It was invented in what is today Turkey during the reign of the Ottoman Empire. Turkish Delight, the term used in Great Britain and the rest of the Western world, found its way to England in the nineteenth century. Turkish Delight has a gummy inside with a sugary powder on the outside. Typically, it is flavored with sugar and rose. We were able to find Turkish Delight imported from Istanbul, Turkey, at a local store. We hope you can find it too and try it. We realize that not all our readers will be able to find it and that our description of its taste and texture are lacking. So, we thought the best way to explain Turkish Delight is to conduct a taste test.

AN UNOFFICIAL SURVEY: TURKISH DELIGHT REVEALED

We decided to get real-life people to try Turkish Delight. How else could we give you an honest rating of the confection! So we went to a local youth group to see what they thought of the sweet. Check out the results . . .

- 84 percent of the test group had never tried Turkish Delight (TD) before

- The average rating for how people thought TD would taste was 7 out of 10

- The actual rating the group gave TD for its taste was 5 out of 10

- In general, almost everyone agreed that it was okay

Here are a few comments about TD that we thought you might find interesting:

- (Liesel) "It tastes like a jelly bean and unfortunately I don't like jelly beans. But I do like the shape, color, and texture, especially the powdery outside in contrast with the silky inside."

- (Jeremy) "I like chocolate much better."

- (Gabbie) "It was really gummy and definitely tasted different than I was expecting, but it's not bad. I don't think I'd get as addicted to it as Edmund did!"

- (Elissa) "It had a good flavor, but the texture is a little strange."

Edmund's Choices

Okay, so you probably will never become a king or queen. Which is not such a big deal now that we have learned what a huge responsibility it is to be royalty. Making decisions for a whole kingdom is hard work. Edmund wanted to be a prince so badly that he could not see that the White Witch did not care about him or his siblings. He trusted someone who showed no sign of being trustworthy. Do you think you would have trusted the White Witch? She offered Edmund two things he greatly desired: Turkish Delight and becoming a prince. Do you think she will follow through on her promises?

SCORING FOR QUEST TO RULE QUIZ

1. A. 2 points

   B. 3 points

   C. 1 point

2. A. 3 points

   B. 2 points

   C. 1 point

3. A. 2 points

   B. 3 points

   C. 1 point

4. A. 1 point

   B. 3 points

   C. 2 points

5. A. 2 points

   B. 1 point

   C. 3 points

6. A. 3 points

   B. 2 points

   C. 1 point

7. A. 1 point

   B. 3 points

   C. 2 points

8. A. 1 point

   B. 2 points

   C. 3 points

9. A. 2 points

   B. 3 points

   C. 1 point

10. A. 2 points

    B. 3 points

    C. 1 point

Logically Speaking

Pinky and Your Brain

Let's talk about the brain for a minute. No, we're not talking about the rodent in the old animated series *Pinky and the Brain* (one which we still remember fondly) who wanted to take over the world. We mean that soft, squishy gray thing inside your head. (Yes, we know. You knew that.)

Your brain, like everyone else's, has two halves called *hemispheres*. One half (the left) is the center of logic and language while the other (right) is the more imaginative, visual half.

Now, wiggle your left pinky. Go on. Wiggle your right. We'll wait.

The left brain controls your right side while your right brain controls your left. Cool, huh?

Ever heard someone called *right-brained* or *left-brained*? That's when you use one half or the other most of the time. But really, both halves of your brain work together. For example, while the right half of your brain recognizes a person's face, the left half of your brain tells you the name of that person. (That's right, ol' what's-his-name.)

As a writer, C. S. Lewis could be very logical and very imaginative. Throughout *LWW*, you can see how logic and imagination work together to create an exciting story. In order to talk about both sides (logic and imagination), we split this chapter into two main parts (logic—chapter 5a—and imagination—chapter 5b). But wait—there's more! We've even given you a bonus chapter, which we'll explain when you get there.

Knock, Knock . . . Who's There?

Remember in chapter 5 of *LWW* when the Professor challenged Peter and Susan after they went to him with their worries about Lucy? When the Professor said, "Either your sister is telling lies, or she is mad, or she is telling the truth," he was using logic. What's logic? When you make reasonable deductions about something based on the evidence you have, you're using logic. For example, if you have four options and you've ruled out Option A, B, or C, you're left with only one choice: D.

C. S. Lewis was a firm believer in using logic to convince people of the truth of his beliefs. A tutor of his named William T. Kirkpatrick, a man his family nicknamed "the Great Knock," inspired him to think deeply before giving an opinion about anything. The Great Knock was a former teacher of Lewis's father and had the task of preparing young Lewis for the Oxford entrance exams. Lewis lived with Kirkpatrick and his wife for over two years, starting in 1914, when he was sixteen.

According to Lewis, Kirkpatrick was almost pure logic. He wouldn't accept an opinion from Lewis like "I like jam" or "This town is wild" without facts that would make the opinion valid (believable or true). Uttering a statement of belief was never enough for the Great Knock. The *why* behind that belief was important. (Like when your mom asks you why you believe that if you don't get some new Skechers before you return to school, *you will simply die*. The *why* is important to her, but maybe you can't put your reasons into words. You just need them *or else you will simply die*.)

The first time C. S. Lewis met the Great Knock, Lewis was humiliated for offering a casual opinion about Great Bookham, the town in which Kirkpatrick lived (in the county of Surrey). When Knock asked Lewis questions to get at the *why* behind his opinion, Lewis didn't exactly know why he felt the way he did. Since Lewis presented no information to back up his opinion, Kirkpatrick felt Lewis had absolutely no right to utter an opinion about the town. Ever have a teacher like that?

As a result of this embarrassment, C. S. Lewis learned to make a thorough investigation about a belief or an idea before making a conclusion about it. This was especially true about Christianity, a subject he learned a lot about by reading or talking to his friends over the years.

For many years, though, logic was a way of life for him. Perhaps some of the appeal of logic came from his mother. After all, she majored in logic and math at Queen's University in Belfast! Lewis, however, had trouble with math (some of us can relate to that). But when he returned to University College at Oxford after fighting in World War II (we'll tell you more about that in chapter 16), he found other challenging subjects to study (the classics, English literature, philosophy, etc.) (Did you get that? Nod if you're still with us.)

TA-DUH!

The Basics on the Classics

You may think of "the Classics" as those books in the bookstore that were written a long time ago (like *Treasure Island* or *The Count of Monte Cristo* or the Baby-sitters Club books—just kidding on the last one). But majoring in classics at college means studying the ancient civilizations of Greece and Rome, their literature, and how it influenced civilizations in the West.

C. S. Lewis had a scholarship to study the classics at Oxford. Studying at prep schools and living with the Great Knock prepared Lewis for his classes at Oxford. He learned to read ancient Greek and Latin and read the works of ancient poets like Homer (a poet who wrote the *Iliad* and the *Odyssey*—narrative poems about the Trojan War; other than that, not much is known about him) and Ovid (a Roman poet whose narrative poem *Metamorphoses* is considered one of the best ever written). (By the way, Lewis also learned Italian and German!)

FYI: Oxford University has the largest classics faculty in the world (or so their Web site tells us). The classics have been taught there for about nine hundred years.

Logic About Narnia

The Professor's words in chapter 5 of *LWW* sound very similar to something C. S. Lewis mentioned in his book *Mere Christianity*. In that book he wrote: "You must make your choice. Either this man [Jesus] was, and is, the Son of God: or else a madman or something worse."[1] He wanted his readers to make a careful investigation of the evidence concerning Christianity instead of a snap judgment. Lewis took his own advice and that of friends like J. R. R. Tolkien, who helped persuade him to believe in God once more (more on that in the next chapter). (Lewis stopped believing in God, especially when he started attending a prep school called Cherbourg in Malvern, in southwest England.)

The Professor wanted Susan and Peter to think deeply before

[1] C. S. Lewis, *Mere Christianity* (New York: The Macmillan Company, 1943), p. 41.

making a conclusion about Lucy. As you know, they were afraid that she had gone out of her mind. (Put yourself in their place. Suppose your sister came to you and said, "I've been to a magical land. All I had to do was walk into my closet." What would you think?) But the Professor didn't want to tell them to believe this way or that way. He wanted them to think for themselves. (Yet, he finally admitted that he believed Lucy *wasn't* crazy.)

If you've read *The Magician's Nephew,* you probably won't wonder why the Professor believed that Lucy was telling the truth. After all, he made the Narnia trip himself. But just think: *The Magician's Nephew* was written after *LWW* was finished. Perhaps as he wrote *LWW,* Lewis wanted to explore why the Professor believed Lucy's story.

All About Professor Kirke

NAME: Digory Kirke

WHERE WE FIRST MEET HIM: Chapter 1 of *LWW*. But we really meet him in *The Magician's Nephew*—he's the nephew.

NICKNAME(S): QUALITIES/PHYSICAL CHARACTERISTICS: In *LWW,* he's described as "odd-looking—a very old man with shaggy white hair." He's known to be "a very remarkable man." He wears glasses and seems to be a logical thinker. Like Lewis, he wonders what kids are learning in school.

CLAIM TO FAME: He's really the first to enter Narnia (unbeknownst to the Pevensies). He owns the house where the Pevensies enter Narnia.

LIKES/LOVES: Unknown, really. He doesn't seem to mind the fact that the Pevensies roam all over his house, so he evidently

---

likes kids to some degree. He certainly doesn't mind being disturbed at times from his work. In chapter 5 of *LWW*, when Susan and Peter interrupt him, he does not yell at them or tell them to go away.

DISLIKES: Unknown. Maybe you can take a guess about some!

NARNIANS WHO SHOW SIGNS OF THINKING LOGICALLY

- Mr. Beaver

- Mrs. Beaver (except about the sewing machine)

- The Dwarf (Okay, he was on the bad side. But he still had a logical mind.)

Everyday Logic

Logic isn't just for professors at Oxford. You probably use some form of it every day. Let's say you want to convince your parents to let you do or buy something. You probably come up with all sorts of reasonable arguments as to why they should let you have the thing you most desire. ("I reeeeeeally need the *World Domination 7* video game, because it will teach me important truths about leadership.")

You can't go too far without running into logic of some kind. Math is based on logic. For example, if $4 \times 4 = 16$, then 4^2 has to be 16, as is 4(4). You do the math!

Using the computer involves taking logical steps. A computer is programmed to "think" logically. If it tells you that you've just performed an illegal function (like trying to install software larger than the space left on your hard drive), it simply won't budge on the matter no matter how much you plead with it.

Some games also emphasize logic. Ever play Clue? In that game, you eliminate the possibilities until you come to the right answer. If you have in your hand the Colonel Mustard card, the knife, and the ballroom card, the murderer couldn't be Colonel Mustard, the murder weapon couldn't be the knife, and the ballroom definitely wasn't the place where the murder took place (even if your cousin tries to cheat). Make sense?

Clue is a simplified version of what jurors go through during trials. Jurors are told to come to a conclusion or verdict based on the evidence. This is not a decision based on feelings, but on cold, hard evidence.

Solve the Logic Puzzle

Now it's your turn. Use logic to solve the following puzzle, based on the situation described below. Read the clues below. The grid will help you store the information in the clues. Mark an X in the box where the information doesn't match the person, the number, or the favorite character listed below. (The chart has already been marked with the information from the first clue, just to give you an idea of how this works.) Use an O when the information matches the person, the number, or the favorite character. Mark an X or an O in the box where the items at the top intersect with the items at the left. If you've marked four Xs in one column, the unmarked box has to be the logical choice (the O).

Here is the situation: Kristin, Martin, Nathan, Megan, and Allan have read *LWW* a certain amount of times (1, 5, 7, 8, or 23 times). Each has a favorite character (Peter, Mrs. Beaver, Edmund, Maugrim, Lucy). Using the clues given below, can you determine how many times each kid has read the book (either once, 5 times, 7 times, 8 times, or 23 times) and which character is his or her favorite?

	1	5	7	8	23	PETER	MRS. BEAVER	EDMUND	MAUGRIM	LUCY
KRISTIN					X					
MARTIN										
NATHAN										
MEGAN					X					
ALLAN										
PETER					
MRS. BEAVER					
EDMUND					
MAUGRIM					
LUCY					

1. Both girls read the book less than 10 times.

2. Allan, whose favorite character is not furry, read the book more than once, but less than 23 times.

3. The person who read the book 5 times has Peter for a favorite character.

4. Megan, who has read the book less than 7 times, does not have a female as a favorite character.

5. The person who read the book 23 times has Lucy for a favorite character.

6. Maugrim is not the favorite character of someone who read the book over 8 times or less than 5.

7. Nathan, who read the book more than once, but less than 8 times, does not like Edmund.

8. Kristin, who read the book more than 5 times, does not like Mrs. Beaver.

LOGIC PUZZLE ANSWERS:

Kristin read the book 8 times and her favorite character is Maugrim.

Martin read the book 23 times and his favorite character is Lucy.

Nathan read the book 7 times and his favorite character is Mrs. Beaver.

Megan read the book once, and her favorite character is Edmund.

Allan read the book 5 times, and his favorite character is Peter.

Imagine That!

A Defeat and a Decision

Do us a favor. Don't think about pink and green striped elephants for five minutes. C'mon, we're begging you. Still thinking about those elephants? We thought so.

Remember how we said that the right half of the brain is the imaginative, visual half? When you think about pink elephants or how a character or a place in a story might look (without looking at a picture of that character or place), you're using the visual part of your brain.

Imagination is one of the most important ingredients of a great story like *LWW*.

Because he was so imaginative himself, C. S. Lewis loved fantasy stories by Edith (also known as E.) Nesbit and Kenneth Grahame (more about them in chapter 5c). Their stories fueled his imagination. But some of the people and events in his life helped to do that, too.

Lewis's friendship with J. R. R. Tolkien (aka Tollers), a friendship that began at Oxford in 1926, was a big influence on Lewis and his writing. Both men had a love of fairy tales and myths.

But Tolkien didn't see these stories as just fun stories to read. He believed that fairy tales showed some truth about God. His beliefs challenged Lewis's way of thinking, not only about fairy tales but about God as well. He helped Lewis to see that believing in God didn't mean that he had to stop being logical. (In fact, after an all-night talk with Tolkien and another friend, Hugo Dyson, in 1931, belief in God made logical sense to Lewis.)

Both also wanted adults to return to reading fairy tales and decided to write the kinds of fairy tales adults would want to read.

Even though some ideas for *LWW* began to form in Lewis's mind (the imaginative side) when he was sixteen (he saw an image of a faun carrying an umbrella), those ideas stayed locked away for many years.

A debate that C. S. Lewis had with a philosopher named Elizabeth Anscombe at the Socratic Club on February 2, 1948, might have helped him to turn back to those ideas. The debate was over a book he wrote called *Miracles*.[1] Anscombe managed to convince even Lewis himself that he could not use only logic (see chapter 5a) to prove that God existed. As a result, Lewis rewrote a chapter

[1] C. S. Lewis, *Miracles: A Preliminary Study* (London: Geoffrey Bles, Ltd., 1947).

of his *Miracles* book. But the debate left him feeling that maybe he needed to write something different. He decided to write the kind of story he would have loved as a child. So, he began work on *LWW*.

In chapter 1 (hey, do you need to look back at it?), we told you that having kids living in his house (the Kilns) during the war also inspired C. S. Lewis to think of stories for kids. He felt sorry for the girls who stayed in his home, because they didn't know many stories. (They hadn't read as many books as he.) He wanted to provide a good story for kids like them to read.

When one of the girls asked him what lay inside a wardrobe, a light bulb went off in his head. He would write a story about a girl who explored a wardrobe. This would be a story "in the tradition of E. Nesbit."[2]

Bad News from a Friend

Lewis began writing a draft of *LWW* in 1939, but did not work on it seriously until 1948. He wasn't idle all that time, however. Aside from teaching at Oxford, he also published several books, including a science fiction trilogy (*Out of the Silent Planet, Perelandra,* and *That Hideous Strength*); *The Great Divorce* (more about that in the next chapter); *The Problem of Pain*; and *The Screwtape Letters*.

Having read and loved Tolkien's stories and having encouraged him to get them published, Lewis wanted his friend to give his opinion about *LWW*. But Tolkien didn't seem to like it. He thought Lewis wrote it too fast and mixed too many fairy-tale creatures from different sources (Greek and Roman mythology) in it. The last straw for Tolkien, however, was the fact

[2] Quoted in *C. S. Lewis: A Biography* by Roger Lancelyn Green and Walter Hooper (London: HarperCollins, 1974), p. 305.

that Lewis even included Father Christmas (more on that in chapter 10)!

Imagine having one of your closest friends tell you how much he or she disliked your work. What would you do? Would you keep going with it? Would you throw it away? C. S. Lewis was so discouraged that he almost stopped writing the story. Perhaps he felt a bit like Lucy in chapter 5 when she faced the disbelief of Peter and Susan upon returning from Narnia.

But There's Good News Too

But someone believed in him—someone else willing to make the journey to Narnia. (No, not literally.) A friend and former student of his at Oxford—Roger Lancelyn Green—also read the story. Green was a writer, whose story adaptations (*King Arthur and His Knights of the Round Table* and *The Adventures of Robin Hood*) would later make him famous (more on story adaptations later). Although he didn't completely agree with everything about *LWW* (he agreed with Tolkien that including Father Christmas wasn't a good idea), Green liked the story for the most part. And he encouraged Lewis to get the book published.

By the way, C. S. Lewis always thought that Roger Lancelyn Green would write a biography of his (Lewis's) life. Sure enough, he did. It was published in 1974—nine years after Lewis's death.

Who or what inspires your imagination? How has a friend helped you to keep working on something you created? (Most important, who is the best person to write a biography of you? Why?)

The 411 on Fairy Tales

Did you know that C. S. Lewis considered his Chronicles of Narnia to be fairy tales?

We'll repeat that: fairy tales. So, what are the characteristics of fairy tales? No one knows for sure. Some people think that fairy tales are stories about fairies. But stories with fairies make up only a small part of fairy tales. Sure, there's "Cinderella," who had a fairy for a godmother, and "Sleeping Beauty"—the story of the enchanted princess whose parents made a grumpy but powerful fairy angry. But then there are stories set within the fairy-tale world that don't directly involve fairies, but have an element of the fantastic about them. (And no, we don't mean your great-uncle Herbert's fishing stories of "the one that got away.") Think about some of your favorite stories.

C. S. Lewis and Tolkien knew this larger fairy-tale world was a world known as Faërie—the land of the fairies and other fairy-tale creatures. In this world, anything is possible.

Now, maybe you thought that certain writers—Andrew Lang, the brothers Grimm, Charles Perrault, Hans Christian Andersen, George Macdonald (more about him in chapter 5c), Roger Lancelyn Green, Tolkien, and of course Lewis—totally made up all of the people or creatures that run around in their worlds (goblins, giants, fauns, satyrs, or other mythical creatures). But some authors adapt (come up with their own variation on) myths or fairy tales that have been around for thousands of years. Andrew Lang, the brothers Grimm, and Roger Lancelyn Green adapted many old stories. Others, like C. S. Lewis and Tolkien, wrote their own original fairy tales, but included some elements from other places (Norse myths, for example).

C. S. Lewis knew how to create a myth and use a myth. To

create his own mythological world, he chose to add creatures from other mythological worlds, creatures like Bacchus—the god of wine in Greek and Roman mythology (he's also called Dionysus)—naiads and dryads, giants, and so on. But he placed them in a world of his own invention. This is what Tolkien objected to.

If you were to write a fairy tale, what fairy-tale creatures would you include? Why?

Sehnsucht

We might as well ask you this now, before we go any further: Are you a fan of fairy tales? You may wonder what the fuss is about fairy tales, if you *don't* like reading them. Judging by the fact that *Shrek 2* was the highest grossing movie of 2004, many people love fairy tales (or at least love tales about smelly ogres)!

So why should anyone bother reading them? For C. S. Lewis, some fairy tales and other tales of the imagination caused him to feel a sense of *sehnsucht*. Before you say, "Bless you" or "Gesundheit" as if we sneezed, allow us to tell you what we mean. *Sehnsucht* is a German word that means "longing." This is a word C. S. Lewis used a lot. For Lewis, this longing was a search for joy, one that raised its head with every story he read that touched his heart (like *Squirrel Nutkin,* believe it or not).

Some fairy tales like *Lord of the Rings* cause people to long after things like heroism, truth, beauty, justice, or heaven. Some can't even explain why they have a certain longing. Think about the last story that touched your heart and imagination. What did it cause you to long for?

Home Sweet Home

There are many historic homes in Great Britain besides the professor's. There are also several historic buildings. For example,

- Buckingham Palace

- Blenheim Palace (Woodstock): home of the 11th Duke of Marlborough and the birthplace of Sir Winston Churchill

- Canterbury Cathedral

- The Kilns (C. S. Lewis's house)

- Palace of Holyroodhouse, Edinburgh (where Queen Elizabeth II lives when she visits Scotland)

- Westminster Abbey, London

- Winchester Cathedral: Jane Austen is buried here (in case you were wondering).

- Woburn Abbey: a Cistercian abbey that includes Wild Animal Kingdom

- York Minster: a large Gothic cathedral known for its stained glass

This Old House

Some of C. S. Lewis's inspiration for *LWW* and his other fairy tales may have come from things he saw every day—things like his house, for instance.

As you know, the Pevensies' adventure in Narnia started in Professor Kirke's house. He had the kind of house that people liked to tour. Old houses often inspire stories and adventures. Lewis's old childhood home (Little Lea) and his later one (the Kilns) probably inspired him to create the Professor's house.

Little did he know that the Kilns would later become a place that tourists would visit. Many people have taken a C. S. Lewis tour of England, which includes a visit to the Kilns and some of Lewis's favorite hangout spots. (Perhaps you've taken one or would like to.)

The C. S. Lewis Foundation of Redlands, California, restored the Kilns in 1998 just before Lewis's one hundredth birthday. (He wasn't around to see it, though, having died in 1963 on the same day that President Kennedy was assassinated: November 22.) Restoring the house took thirteen years.[3]

What kind of house do you live in? Have you explored it like we suggested in chapter 1? After exploring her house, Carrie found one of her kitten Sassie's baby teeth. What have you found?

𝔄nd 𝔑ow, a 𝔚ord 𝔄bout 𝔄rmor

In many tales of knights (but not days—get it? Knights, nights? Okay, maybe that's not a winner), you can't help but notice armor. Would a big, fancy historic house be worth anything without a suit of armor or two in its halls? (Okay, maybe *some* historic houses didn't have armor and are still worth quite a lot.) Professor Kirke's home had armor. Many historic homes in Great Britain have armor on display. Some of these pieces of armor were family heirlooms. Maybe you've seen some armor in a museum.

---

[3] If you'd like more information about this, we read a cool story at http://www.christianitytoday.com/tc/8r1/8r1039.html. But as we mentioned in chapter 3, you might check with your parents before checking it out.

Mail (hauberk)   Mail (snail)

Since you probably aren't going to a museum or one of those fancy homes anytime soon and since we think armor is cool (would you agree?), we've decided to give you a very brief history of armor right in the pages of this book. (You're welcome.)

Armor has been around in some form for thousands of years. The first kind of armor was a shirt of linked rings called *mail* that was either waist-length or knee-length. The knee-length mail shirt was called a *hauberk* or *habergeon*.

But these shirts of mail didn't protect the legs. So, during the twelfth century, many soldiers began wearing mail pieces attached by leather on the front of their legs. If you've read. *The Horse and His Boy,* you've probably seen pictures of Aravis, the Tarkheena, wearing a mail shirt and mail leggings. (If you saw any of the *Lord of the Rings* movies, directed by Peter Jackson, you saw a lot of mail.)

Some of the armor you see in museums came about slowly in the thirteenth century as pieces of armor (like a helm or gauntlets) were layered on top of the mail.

In the fifteenth century, armor made of metal plates was more common. Some German and Italian craftsmen were well known

Helm for a knight   Helm for a ship

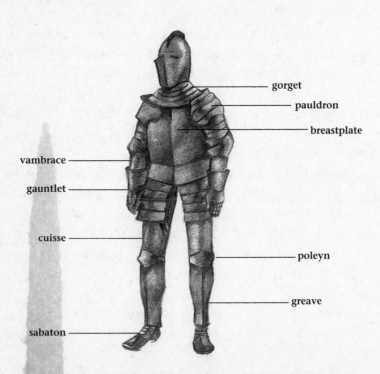

Sixteenth-century armor on display at the Metropolitan Museum of Art in New York City

for making armor. But a full set of armor was very expensive. The average soldier could not afford it.

COAT OF ARMS

If you know anything about knights or royalty, you know many had a coat of arms on their breastplate or shield. A coat of arms is a picture that identified a knight or king or described his status. Having a coat of arms was considered "cool" back then. A coat of arms could be passed down in a family from one generation to the next.

During the Crusades (the wars fought for Jerusalem by soldiers from different countries in Europe against Muslim soldiers), many knights wore a cross marked on their shields or *surcoats* (long, sleeveless tunics) as a way of identifying their cause.

A coat of arms has many parts: a shield, helm (we showed you a picture of one), mantling, supporters (usually two animals standing on either side of the shield), and a wreath (not the Christmas kind). The main part is the shield. The picture or color chosen for a shield always has a meaning. The pictures are called *charges*. Usually, an animal (bear, boar, dragon, eagle, griffin, horse, or lion) is shown in one of several battle poses (*rampant:* standing on its hind legs; *couchant:* lying down; *rampant guardant:* on hind legs facing the viewer; *passant:* walking; *sejant:* sitting).

The colors used were *azure* (royal blue), *gules* (red), *vert* (emerald green), *sable* (black), *purpure* (royal purple), *or* (gold), and *argent* (silver).

C. S. Lewis undoubtedly knew about charges. Before Peter's first battle in Narnia (chapter 12 in *LWW*), Father Christmas gave him a sword and a shield with a red lion on it (see chapter 10). The lion, which represented Aslan, had a rampant pose. Perhaps it looked similar to the shield that Henry I (England's king, 1100–35) gave his son-in-law, Geoffrey of Anjou, in 1127 after knighting him.

The rampant lion also could be found on Aslan's standard (his flag) in chapter 12.

If you were to create your own coat of arms, what would it look like? Use your imagination!

Arms given by Henry I, King of England

Arms—the first arms created

The Imaginers

In chapter 6 of *LWW,* remember what Susan said about the fur coats? Okay, we'll tell you. She said that by wearing them as they explored Narnia, her siblings weren't actually taking them *out* of the wardrobe. Technically, they were still *in* the wardrobe.

Well, technically, we're still in chapter 5 of *this* book. That's right: chapter 5. Back in 5a, we told you about the logical part of C. S. Lewis's mind—the part that caused him to be really good in an argument. And in 5b, we started telling you about C. S. Lewis's imagination—the part that helped him create Narnia.

This chapter is all about some of the fantasy writers—you probably know them all—who inspired Lewis. Although there were many authors whose books C. S. Lewis found delightful and inspiring, we selected only a few of the ones he seemed to mention most often. If you really want to understand how he came to write *LWW* and the rest of the Chronicles of Narnia, the best place to start is here among these fine writers, people like

Kenneth Grahame (1859–1932)

Grahame's *The Wind in the Willows* (have you read it?), a tale of talking animals published in 1908, became a life-long favorite of Lewis. Makes sense, doesn't it, since our friend Mr. Lewis developed his own "Animal-land" when he was a boy. (Remember that from the Introduction?) Yet Lewis didn't read *The Wind in the Willows* until he was an adult (like some of us).

Grahame was born in Scotland, but raised in Berkshire, a county in the south of England. Although he worked as a banker, he kept writing stories. (Like Lewis, he was both logical and imaginative, huh?) He loved the river, just as Rat, one of his main characters, loves the river in *Wind in the Willows*. (Lewis also loved being in or near water. You can tell that by the way he describes the sea in chapter 17 of *LWW*.) Grahame loved "messing about in boats," as Rat would say. (How about you?) He also loved kids—especially his son Alistair, for whom he wrote *Willows*.

Living with his grandmother in her country house helped inspire Grahame to write the book that kids and adults (including us) have loved for many years. Does that sound familiar? Living in a big house out in the country helped inspire C. S. Lewis, too. (And, like Lewis, Grahame's mom died when he was a kid.)

In his essay "On Stories,"[1] C. S. Lewis mentions Toad, who is one of the most memorable and mischievous characters in the book (would you agree?) and why Grahame probably chose to make his character a toad as opposed to a man. In another essay, "On Three Ways of Writing for Children," in the same book he explains why Mr. Badger is such an enduringly popular character. (Well, he is.)

In his book *The Four Loves*,[2] C. S. Lewis talks about the friendship of Rat, Mole, Badger, and Toad, and how it helped make the story great (just as the Pevensies' love for each other and for Aslan makes *LWW* great). Maybe your friendships make your story—your life—great, too.

---

[1] This essay can be found in C. S. Lewis's book, *On Stories and Other Essays on Literature*, ed. Walter Hooper (New York: Harcourt Brace Jovanovich, 1982).
[2] C. S. Lewis, *The Four Loves* (London: Geoffrey Bles, Ltd., 1960; New York: Harcourt, Brace and World, Inc. 1960).

George Macdonald (1824–1905)

In the preface (the short piece at the beginning of a book that an author writes to introduce a book, however, it's not an introduction like the one at the beginning of this book) to an anthology of George Macdonald's stories,[3] C. S. Lewis said, "I have never concealed the fact that I regarded him as my master." *Whoa!* you might say, *Just who* is *this guy?* He's the guy who wrote *The Princess and the Goblin, The Princess and Curdie, At the Back of the North Wind,* shorter fairy tales like "The Light Princess," "The Wise Woman, or the Lost Princess," and many others. But reading Macdonald's fantasy book *Phantastes* (published in 1858) back in 1916 had a huge impact on Lewis's imagination. (To think, he picked up an old copy of the book by chance at a bookstall.)

George Macdonald, a former English professor and minister, wrote many books (about fifty) and poems, and even encouraged a family friend, Lewis Carroll, to get his own novel published: *Alice in Wonderland.* (Aren't you glad he did?)

C. S. Lewis appreciated the fact that this Scottish-born author and father of eleven kids combined Christian faith and myths in his stories and kept them interesting at the same time. (We appreciate that as well.) Macdonald's views on myths (that truth can be found in them) helped change Lewis's writing life.

Lewis and Macdonald have a number of things in common. For one thing, Macdonald also grieved over the death of his mother at a young age (eight). Also Like C. S. Lewis, Macdonald never claimed to write just for kids. (Hey, no offense! He wanted people of *all* ages to enjoy his stories.) But his stories inspired many fantasy writers of the twentieth century. Perhaps his stories have inspired you as well.

As proof of Macdonald's influence on Lewis's life, George

---

[3] Geoffrey Bles published the anthology in 1946. William B. Eerdmans published an edition of *Phantastes* in 2000.

Macdonald pops up as a character in Lewis's book, *The Great Divorce* (which is not about divorce). He has a conversation with the main character—the narrator of the story—and answers some of the questions Lewis himself asked at one point or another (about the link between myths and faith; about heaven). In fact, the narrator of the story tells Macdonald that he bought a copy of *Phantastes,* which made an impact on his life. This was Lewis's experience in real life.

Interestingly enough, Lewis didn't think that Macdonald was the best writer he ever read. But he kept reading his books, because of his appreciation of Macdonald's imagination and skill at teaching truth through fairy tales.

Edith Nesbit (1858–1924)

Better known as E. Nesbit
Take an English tomboy educated in France who later became the mother of five children and the friend of H. G. Wells (author of *The Time Machine*) and what do you get? You get E. Nesbit, the woman who later inspired Lewis to write a book "in the tradition of E. Nesbit."

Nesbit wrote a series of books about two families of kids. The first family—Cyril, Anthea, Robert, and Jane (and their baby brother, whom they've nicknamed "the Lamb")—are the stars of *Five Children and It, The Phoenix and the Carpet,* and *The Amulet.* These stories involve a sand fairy (a Psammead) that grants wishes that cause a great deal of trouble. The second family, the six Bastables, stars in *The Story of the Treasure Seekers, The Wouldbe-goods* and other books. Their stories are less fantastic than the sand fairy stories and more realistic. (Nesbit's stories are either fantastic or realistic.)

E. Nesbit's stories are full of adventure and older brothers who like to tease younger sisters. (Just like Edmund!)

As he explained in an essay,[4] Lewis read some of Nesbit's stories when he was in his late twenties. But during his childhood, Nesbit's stories of the five children were serialized in a magazine called *The Strand. The Amulet* was a particular favorite of Lewis. If you read *The Amulet,* maybe you noticed that Cyril and his siblings are in the same order age-wise as the Pevensies. (We sure did.)

AGE ORDER

Cyril	Peter
Anthea	Susan
Robert	Edmund
Jane	Lucy

E. Nesbit wrote other novels besides the ones above. All in all, she wrote forty-four (including *The Enchanted Castle,* which involves another group of kids, and *The House of Arden*). She probably wouldn't have considered herself a children's book author. No, she wrote books *about* kids, but not necessarily *just* for kids (although if kids read her books, she wouldn't have screamed). Like Lewis, Grahame, and Macdonald, she hoped that anyone of any age could enjoy her books. Do you? (You can find her books at your local library.)

FYI: If you've read any of Edward Eager's books, you'll know that E. Nesbit inspired him, too.

---

[4] "On Three Ways of Writing for Children," in *On Stories and Other Essays on Literature.*

Beatrix Potter (1866–1943)

You may know her as the author/illustrator of *The Tale of Peter Rabbit* and other young children's books. But would you expect her to be a favorite author of C. S. Lewis? He loved her "dressed animal" stories and named *The Tale of Squirrel Nutkin* as one of his favorites.[5] (It was published when he was five!) Through that book, Lewis came to realize his love for autumn.

Beatrix Potter, who was born in South Kensington, London, shared a love of animals with her brother Bertram. They had quite a few animals around to study, sketch, photograph, and examine under a microscope.

Beatrix also loved the country, especially the area around Lakeland, where her family spent their vacations. This natural setting inspired her in the way that Lewis's childhood home did.

Unlike C. S. Lewis or her brother, Beatrix wasn't allowed to go to school. She had a governess, but no formal art training. But she loved art. (Being left alone a lot like Lewis, especially when her brother was sent to school, gave her plenty of time to paint.) Her father, an amateur artist, would take her to exhibitions by famous artists. She kept a journal in her own made-up code for many years. (Lewis also kept a journal.)

Her books started as illustrated letters written to entertain the kids of her former governess. In one letter to a sick child, she told the story of Peter Rabbit. But when she tried to get the story published, she was rejected until she decided to self-publish it. After the self-published books sold out, Frederick Warne & Company— one of many publishers that previously rejected her book— decided to take a second look at her Peter Rabbit story. The rest is history.

[5] He mentions this in his autobiography, *Surprised by Joy*.

John Ronald Reuel Tolkien (1892–1973)

Better known as J. R. R. Tolkien

We've mentioned him before (see chapter 5b), but he certainly belongs here among the people who influenced C. S. Lewis's imagination. Many, many books have been written about Tolkien, because of the worldwide success of the *Lord of the Rings* trilogy (favorites of ours) and *The Hobbit*.

Like Lewis, Tolkien loved Norse myths and other types of fairy stories. (Norse myths are tales and poems from Scandinavia wayyyyy back during the twelfth century or so. Old Norse is a combination of Norwegian, Icelandic, and Faerose.) He's the one who also told Lewis that truths about God can be found in fairy stories. Also like Lewis and Macdonald, Tolkien believed that stories written for one age group (say, kids) weren't very good stories.

His love of languages (Welsh, Finnish, German) led him to create several languages of his own (like the languages of the elves in *Lord of the Rings*). Since he had the languages, he decided to create a world to explain the use of those languages.

Like Lewis, he fought in World War I at the rank of second lieutenant. (Lewis also was a second lieutenant. We discuss this more in chapter 16. Can you wait that long? If not, skip to that chapter right now! Be sure to mark your place so that you know to come back here when you're done.) Unlike Lewis, he married and finished his degree at Oxford before going to war. (He studied the classics, Old English, Germanic languages, English literature, and philology—the study of languages. You see, now, what he had in common with Lewis.)

Although he was not wounded, he was ill with trench fever. (Lewis had that too; see chapter 16.) Unfortunately, during that war, most of his friends were killed. But living through two wars helped him give shape to the world that readers would come to know as Middle Earth—with all of its history.

The Inklings

We could not possibly leave this chapter without talking a little bit about the Inklings. This group met weekly (sometimes on Monday or Tuesday mornings, other times on Thursday evenings) during the 1930s and '40s and consisted of Lewis, Tolkien, and Charles Williams; Owed Barfield (Lewis was his daughter's godfather); Warren Lewis; Nevill Coghill (an Oxford professor); John Wain (not to be confused with John Wayne, the American actor famous for westerns—this is John Wain, the English poet and novelist); Gervase Mathews (a lecturer at Oxford); Hugo Dyson (whose talk with Lewis along with Tolkien helped Lewis believe in God once again); Robert "Humphrey" Havard (another lecturer, who also was Lewis's and Warren's doctor); Lord David Cecil (an Oxford professor); and others, including Tolkien's son Christopher. Some friends and fellow writers like Eric Rucker Eddison (whose novel *The Worm Ouroboros* also was a favorite of Lewis's) and Dorothy Sayers (the Lord Peter Wimsey mystery series) made guest appearances.

The Inklings liked hanging out together and hoped to encourage each other in their writing. During these meetings, someone would read a portion of his work. Tolkien read parts of *Lord of the Rings*. Lewis read part of his books (like *The Problem of Pain,* which he dedicated to the Inklings). The Inklings didn't always agree. Some of the members liked some stories better than others. But together they produced books that made a difference in their world and helped inspire countless other writers.

Years later (after working on the *Oxford English Dictionary*), when he returned to Oxford as a professor of Anglo-Saxon (Old English), Tolkien and Lewis founded a writers' group called the Inklings.

So, there you have it: the people who helped influence C. S. Lewis. Think about your favorite writers. Maybe they'll inspire you to do something cool someday.

CHAPTER SIX

Over the River and Through the Woods

Sing with us now, "Over the river and through the woods to grandmother's house we gooooooo!" We couldn't help thinking of the familiar song as we read chapter 6 of *LWW* (even though the river was not crossed until chapter 7).

If you've read as many fairy tales and adventure stories as we have, you probably notice that many characters seem to wind up in woods of some kind. There's

- Hansel and Gretel, who left a trail of bread crumbs to help them get through the forest. (You can find this story in the collection of Grimms' fairy tales.)

- A princess, who met a frog in the woods who later turned into a prince (another of the fairy tales by the brothers Grimm)

- Snow White, who got lost in the woods after the hunter, who was sent by the envious queen to kill her, told her to run away.

- Little Red Riding Hood, who heads to Granny's house in the woods, but meets a certain wolf.

- Robin Hood and his merry men, who were forced to live in Sherwood Forest when their homes were taken away from them.

- Frodo, Sam, Merry, and Pippin, who traveled through the Old Forest in *Fellowship of the Ring* (Book 1 of *The Lord of the Rings* trilogy; or simply *The Lord of the Rings* if you have all three stories in one volume).

- Aragorn, Gimli, Legolas, Merry, and Pippin, who wound up in Fangorn Forest at different times in *The Two Towers* (Book 2 of *The Lord of the Rings*).

There's even a famous musical called *Into the Woods,* which features characters from different fairy tales wandering through the woods. As the characters walk through the woods, we get to see their personalities in action.

There's someone else you might have found wandering in the woods (had you been alive in his day): C. S. Lewis. He loved the country and loved a good hike. He especially loved to take walking tours with his brother and friends. So it's no wonder that his characters wound up in the woods (and excited to be there) when they unexpectedly found themselves in Narnia. Lucy and Edmund had been there before. At last, all had arrived in this strange kingdom. Their different reactions upon arriving in the woods caused us to consider how different each one was from the other. So, we couldn't help coming up with a quiz based on the four Pevensies. Ready to take it? We thought you would be.

Which Pevensie Are You Most Like?

Are you a Peter? A Susan? An Edmund? A Lucy? Take this quiz and see. To find out your score, go to the end of the chapter.

1. If you were to suddenly find yourself in the woods in a strange country, you would:
   A. insist on exploring it.
   B. pretend to be an Arctic explorer.
   C. look for a landmark or a friend to be with.
   D. make sure everyone with you is dressed warmly first.

2. When friends want to hang out with you, you're usually the one who:
   A. comes up with the plan for what you're going to do.
   B. looks for adventure wherever it may find you.
   C. gives an opinion about any plans they make.
   D. goes along with whatever they want to do.

3. When you feel scared, you usually:
   A. fight the fear and do what you have to do.
   B. tell someone that you're scared.
   C. make everyone else think he or she is the one who's scared, not you.
   D. think of a practical way to get over it.

4. If a friend or sibling did something that you didn't like, you would:
   A. tell him or her to get his/her act together or else!
   B. avoid him/her for a while.
   C. make plans to get even.
   D. ask him/her to please try to get along.

5. You consider yourself to be:
   A. the one who needs to be in charge. Hey, it's a gift.
   B. just an ordinary kid.
   C. smarter than the average human.
   D. someone others depend on.

6. If someone you loved was hurting, you would:
   A. tell him/her to keep his/her chin up.
   B. want to be near him/her to help comfort.
   C. feel embarrassed and wish he/she would get over it.
   D. ask first before offering comfort.

7. If you did wrong to someone, you would:
   A. immediately admit that you're wrong and try to make it right.
   B. ask for forgiveness.
   C. first act like you didn't do anything wrong, then finally admit that you did.
   D. try to make peace and promise to understand his/her point of view next time.

8. In a battle situation, you would:
   A. lead the charge into battle.
   B. be the one to offer comfort to the soldiers who fought.
   C. come up with the strategy for winning the battle.
   D. alert others to the battle.

(See end of chapter for scoring.)

Well, which Pevensie are you most like? Was that the result that you expected? Why or why not?

Now that you've taken that quiz, let's move on to some of the sights you might see during a walk in the woods of Narnia. Since walks occur in more than one chapter of Narnia (chapters 6, 9, 10, 11, 12, and 15, for instance), we decided to combine all of the information in this handy chapter.

A Few Good Flowers and Trees

You can't walk through woods without seeing plants and trees (Duh). In various chapters of *LWW,* Lewis mentions several kinds of plants and trees in Narnia: beech, oak, silver birch, larch, elm, fir, laburnum, and cherry, plus flowers like bluebells, celandine, primroses, and crocuses, and bushes like flowering currant and hawthorn.

A writer usually writes about what he or she knows. As a gardener, Lewis was undoubtedly familiar with these plants and trees. We're going to tell you a little bit about them.[1]

TREES

BEECH Have you seen a beech tree? When it comes to trees in Great Britain, many people think of beech trees, and not just because of the furniture made from them. You see, beech trees are native to the south of England. When we say *native,* we really mean a longer word—*indigenous.* That means a tree naturally grows there. It wasn't brought there by anyone and forced into the ecosystem.

There are several kinds of beech trees. Beech trees have gray bark, can grow over 100 feet, and can live about 250 years! They're also deciduous trees. This means their leaves fall off in the fall, but they gain new ones in the spring.

And they're catkin-bearing trees. What are catkins? They're clusters of flowers that—believe it or not—are considered male or female.

---

[1] A great site for information about English plants and trees is that of the Royal Forestry Society of England, Wales, and Northern Ireland: http://www.rfs.org.uk. If you can't get there, check out *Trees & Bushes of Europe* by Oleg Polunn with drawings by Barbara Everard (New York: Oxford University Press). (Check with your parents before going online.)

CHERRY A bird cherry tree native to Great Britain has white, almond-scented flowers and black, bitter-tasting berries. (You don't want to eat those.) A wild cherry tree (not to be confused with the bubble gum flavor), on the other hand, has red fruit that is sometimes sweet and sometimes bitter. It can be found in woods and can grow to a height of over 60 feet. And no, George Washington did not chop one down in Narnia.

ELM Elms can be found all over the United States. But several kinds of elms can be found in Europe. The species of tree that's probably the most widely found there is the English elm (*Ulmus procera*—amaze your friends with your knowledge of Latin scientific names). The elm is a deciduous tree with gray or brown bark. Alas, this tree has an enemy—Dutch elm disease.

FIR C. S. Lewis was not specific about the type of firs in Narnia. Perhaps they're Douglas firs or Giant firs. Both kinds of trees, which are part of the pine family, are found in Europe.

Firs are conifers. That means they are cone-bearing trees.

The Douglas fir (also called the Oregon pine) was named after a Scottish botanist named David Douglas. But it is not native to Great Britain. Douglas brought it to Scotland in 1827.

In the Rocky Mountains, you can see plenty of Douglas firs. These trees only reach a height of about 130 feet in the Rockies, but only about 150–180 feet in Great Britain.

Traditionally, the Douglas fir has been used for Christmas trees.

LABURNUM This small flowering, deciduous tree (about 22 feet high) is indigenous to Northern Europe. It can be found in forests in the mountains. Although it produces beautiful yellow flowers that hang down in clusters, they're poisonous.

LARCHES The larch is another tree people usually think of when they think of Great Britain. That's probably because you can find a lot of them there. But this tree isn't native to Great Britain. Two kinds were introduced: Japanese larches and European larches (hybrid larch trees—trees bred from European and Japanese larches—also exist). The European larch comes from—you guessed it—other parts of Europe, and the Japanese larch comes from Japan.

Although the larch is a conifer tree, it sheds its leaves in the fall—something conifers usually don't do. Guess you could call it an uncommon conifer.

OAK You've undoubtedly seen oak trees. The United States has many kinds. Maybe you've even sat on chairs or at tables made from oaks.

There are many forests of oaks and beeches in Europe. The common oak is the one you see the most there. (Guess that's why it's called common.)

The common oak (also known as the English oak or the pedunculate oak) can grow over 100 feet.

An oak tree has the reputation for being a "mighty" tree. Wondering why? Because they can reach a height of over 100 feet in some forests and live for 1,000 years (even though they take ages to grow)!

To think that this huge, spreading tree gets its start from a little acorn. It's also a distant relative of the beech tree (on its mother's side . . . just kidding).

SILVER BIRCH In chapter 11 of *LWW*, Lewis mentions quite a few trees, including silver birches. You can find plenty of silver birch trees in England and other parts of Europe. These conifer trees, which are known for their white bark, can reach a height of 98 feet.

Like the beech, these deciduous trees produce catkins (female).

FLOWERS

BLUEBELLS Have you ever seen a carpet of bluebells? There are woods in England where bluebells grow wild. There are so many of them, they look like a carpet.

Bluebells, which are also called hyacinths, are native to Great Britain. They're called bluebell because of their bell shape and color.

CELANDINE There are two different types of celandine: the greater celandine and the lesser celandine. We're not exactly sure which one C. S. Lewis refers to. Both have small yellow flowers, even though they are not two types of the same plant. Lesser celandine flowers have eight small petals, while greater celandine flowers have about four. Both are probably native to the United Kingdom.

In Europe and in the United States the greater celandine (just the leaves and flowers, not the bulb) is used to treat indigestion and warts. In a plant lore book,[2] we discovered that celandine has been used as a skin cleanser (but don't run out and find any to rub on your face).

CROCUS C. S. Lewis mentions different colors of crocuses: gold, purple, and white. There are probably seventy-five different kinds of crocuses. The crocus is usually one of the first flowers of spring. A crocus is part of the iris family of flowers. But it isn't native to England; it was brought there from France.

Crocuses that grow in the fall and the spring are of different types. The ones in Narnia are undoubtedly the spring variety.

There are a number of myths about crocuses, including the one about a shepherd boy named Crocus, who fell in love with a nymph and wound up turned into a flower.

PRIMROSE This five-petal flower is usually one of the first to spring up in the spring. About five hundred different kinds of primroses

---

[2] Roy Vickery, *A Dictionary of Plant-Lore* (London: Oxford University Press, 1995).

exist. Some are native to Great Britain; they prefer the cooler regions of the hills.

BUSHES

FLOWERING CURRANT This could be the flowering currant named for Edward VII, King of Great Britain and Ireland (1901–10), that produces black berries in the fall. This shrub is not native to Great Britain. It was brought over in the early nineteenth century.

HAWTHORN (MAY TREE) Hawthorn, a deciduous shrub and also a small tree, is pretty common in England. (It's called whitethorn in Ireland.) Birds eat the red hawthorn berries in the winter.

Over the centuries there have been many superstitions about hawthorns in different regions in the UK. Some people believed that hawthorns were fairy trees. Others believed that bad things would happen if hawthorn blossoms were brought inside the home.

Birds in Narnia and Other Places

Remember how the Pevensies talked about the birds in Narnia as they walked through the woods? Peter said that robins were usually good in stories. So, which are the "good" and the "bad" birds in Narnia and in other stories?

CROWS

Crows and ravens are sometimes used interchangeably in stories. They're from the same family of birds, after all (*Corvidae*). But in reality, ravens are larger than crows.

Crows have a bad reputation, except in the Narnia stories. In other stories they're scavengers, animals that tease others, or they work for the wrong people. In *The Wonderful Wizard of Oz*, the Wicked Witch of the West sent crows to harm Dorothy and her friends. In Tolkien's *Lord of the Rings* trilogy, crows were spies of Saruman the wizard, who turned as bad as mayonnaise gets in the sun.

We don't hear of any crows in *LWW* (except possibly in an illustration), but there are crows in Narnia. After all, a jackdaw (a Eurasian crow), a character in *The Magician's Nephew*, makes the first joke in Narnia. Crows are probably on the side of good in Narnia, for the most part.

EAGLES

They're usually heroic, majestic birds that happen to be fierce fighters. In *LWW*, eagles are sent to the rescue of Edmund. Also, in Tolkien's *Lord of the Rings* series and *The Hobbit*, the eagles come to the rescue more than once in the nick of time. Still, you don't want to get on their bad side.

KINGFISHERS

In chapter 12, the Pevensies notice a kingfisher in Narnia—a sign of the return of spring. Other than the mention of it, there's nothing to show that this bird is any different from kingfishers in our world. Since the piping of the kingfisher is usually a happy sound, these birds are probably on the side of good.

In a Roman myth called "Ceyx and Alcyone," written by the poet Ovid, Ceyx and his wife Alcyone were transformed into kingfishers, which is also known as the halcyon. But the halcyon in Greek and Roman myths has some characteristics that aren't exactly like the kingfisher in real life. They hang around sea nymphs for one thing and lay eggs in the winter.[3]

---

[3] If you're looking for a book on birds in myths, check out *The Life and Lore of the Bird: In Nature, Art, Myth, and Literature* by Edward A. Armstrong (New York: Crown, 1975).

The halcyon, like the dove, is a symbol of peace in some stories. Shakespeare also mentions the halcyon that way in some of his plays (see *Henry IV,* Part I; and *King Lear*).

OWLS

These birds get a lot of attention nowadays thanks to J. K. Rowling's Harry Potter stories. In many stories, they're thought to be wise. They have that reputation in Narnia.

Certain species of owls (like barn owls) were linked to witches in stories, particularly during the Middle Ages. Barn owls also are known as ghost owls. They exist on every continent in the world except Antarctica.

The tawny owl (sometimes called a hoot owl), one of Britain's most common birds of prey, pops up in a number of fairy tales.

PELICANS

These waterbirds (some of which have a ten-foot wingspan!) were on Aslan's side, or at least one was, judging by chapter 12. They have good reputations in stories. After all, Nigel the brown pelican saved the day in *Finding Nemo*.

In medieval times, the pelican was believed to be a symbol of self-sacrifice and of Christ. Self-sacrificing pelicans are mentioned in two of Shakespeare's plays, *Hamlet* and *Richard II*.

RAVENS

Ever read the poem *The Raven* by Edgar Allan Poe? Creepy, huh? Well, that's the view of ravens in stories for the most part. They're usually seen as omens of danger or death in Celtic legends. They were also used as messengers in those legends.

A trickster in Native American myths often takes the form of a raven—another reason why people might view the raven in a negative way.

Sometimes innocent people are turned into ravens. That's what happens in the story "The Raven," by the brothers Grimm.

Sallow pad, a raven of good reputation, turns up in *The Horse and His Boy*.

THRUSHES

Also in chapter 12 of *LWW*, the Pevensies noticed a thrush in Narnia (a sign of the return of spring). The song of the thrush is usually a happy sound, as is the case here.

"King Thrushbeard" is one of the better-known stories involving a thrush. In that story, a spoiled princess makes fun of a suitor, claiming that he has a chin as pointed as the beak of a thrush. (The quickest way to lose a suitor.)

On Your Mark, Get Set, Go!

When you wander through woods, you need to know how to navigate. Otherwise, you could wander for years and never get out.

Two useful tools to use in navigation are a compass and a map. The Pevensies didn't have a compass or a map. Instead, they had landmarks like Mr. Tumnus's cave and the lamppost to help them find their way through the woods. Mainly, they relied on Lucy, who oriented herself by looking for familiar trees and stumps. Later, in chapter 7, they had a guide—Mr. Beaver.

If you happened to be in Narnia with a compass and a map (like, say, the map in *LWW*), you could orient yourself by placing your compass on the map at your starting point, and then moving the compass housing to align its orienting lines with the meridian lines on the map (the longitudinal lines that point north).

As you know, the red part of the compass needle usually points north. Once you take the compass off the map, move yourself in the direction of the arrow on the compass. Before moving, however, pick out a spot in front of you (a tree in the distance or a rock formation) and head in that direction. Look for algae on the sides of trees as a way to find north.[4]

PEVENSIE QUIZ ANSWERS

Mostly A's—Face it, you're Peter. You like being in charge and might seem a little bossy to some. But it's time they knew what you know: that you're right most of the time.

Mostly B's—You're Lucy all the way. You like adventure, but dislike family conflict.

Mostly C's—You're like Edmund, dude. You like having your own way, which is a weakness. Yet when you're wrong, you finally come around in the end.

Mostly D's—You're like Susan: the peacemaker of the family. Still, you're cautious about helping out sometimes.

[4] A good site for learning to use a compass is one by Kjetil Kjernsmo: http://www.learn-orienteering.org/old/lesson2.html. Before you check it out, check with your parents!

CHAPTER SEVEN

Busy as a Beaver

A Bit About Beavers

Who are your favorite characters in *LWW*? Aslan? Lucy? Mr. Tumnus? The Beavers are favorites of at least one of us (Linda).

Remember back in the Introduction (if you haven't read it, now's your chance), we talked about C. S. Lewis's fondness for writing stories about "dressed animals"? Throughout the Narnia stories, you can see what a big part animals play.

As you read how the Pevensies met Mr. and Mrs. Beaver in *LWW*, perhaps like us you wondered how beavers in our world are similar to or different from beavers in Narnia. (Or perhaps you just fixed yourself a peanut butter and jelly sandwich and didn't think about it at all.)

Before we compare and contrast beavers in both worlds (for those of you who *want* to know), here's your chance to test your knowledge about beavers in our world and in Narnia. There are two ways you can do this. You can take the novice quiz (if you want a light challenge) or the intermediate quiz (if you're up for a bigger challenge). Warning: If you decide to take both quizzes, you might run into some of the same questions. It's best to take one or the other. Also, please take the quiz before reading the rest of this chapter.

Novice Quiz

1. Beavers build
   A. Condos.
   B. Dams.
   C. Lodges.
   D. B and C above.

Okay. That was an easy one. Next!

2. A beaver is what kind of animal?
   A. Reptile
   B. Rodent
   C. Marsupial
   D. Monotreme (an egg-laying mammal)

3. Among this group of animals (the answer to #2), beavers are the ____ largest.
   A. First
   B. Second
   C. Third
   D. Fourth

4. The average adult beaver weighs about
   A. 10–20 pounds.
   B. 25–40 pounds.
   C. 45–60 pounds.
   D. Over 60 pounds.

5. The fact that a beaver's eyes, nose, and ears are positioned high on its head means what exactly?

A. They don't have good peripheral (side) vision, but their senses of smell and hearing are good.

B. They're built for life in the water.

C. Nothing really; this is just a useful fact about beavers.

6. Beavers are known for having which kind of tail?
   A. A flat, oval tail
   B. Long, bushy tail
   C. Long, striped tail
   D. Flat, rectangular tail

7. Beavers like to eat
   A. twigs and bark.
   B. skunk cabbage.
   C. grass.
   D. all of the above.

8. Beavers are ready to leave home and start a family at the age of
   A. two.
   B. three.
   C. four.
   D. five.

Have you checked your answers yet? How'd you do?

Intermediate Quiz

You can answer a question six ways. Is it . . .

- true for Narnian Beavers only? Mark TNB

- true for Beavers in our world only? Mark TBW

- false for Narnian Beavers? Mark FNB

- false for Beavers in our world? Mark FBW

- true for both? Mark TB

- false for both? Mark FB

Ready? Go! (You can check your answers at the end of the chapter)

1. Beavers build dams and live in lodges.
   TNB   TBW   FNB   FBW   TB   FB

2. A beaver is a monotreme (an egg-laying mammal).
   TNB   TBW   FNB   FBW   TB   FB

3. Beavers love to eat fish.
   TNB   TBW   FNB   FBW   TB   FB

4. For a beaver, a wolf is a predator.
   TNB   TBW   FNB   FBW   TB   FB

5. A beaver will usually stay in one home from one season to the next.
   TNB   TBW   FNB   FBW   TB   FB

6. When chased by a predator, a beaver usually hides in a cave.
   TNB   TBW   FNB   FBW   TB   FB

7. Because some beavers' dams are so strongly built, you can walk across them.
   TNB   TBW   FNB   FBW   TB   FB

8. Beavers use sticks and mud to build their homes.

   TNB   TBW   FNB   FBW   TB   FB

9. A beaver stores some food underwater to eat during the winter.

   TNB   TBW   FNB   FBW   TB   FB

10. A beaver's winter diet is mostly bark—not the wood itself.

    TNB   TBW   FNB   FBW   TB   FB

11. Beavers often have to fight other animals or beavers to survive.

    TNB   TBW   FNB   FBW   TB   FB

12. A beaver's home has only one entrance—on top of the dam.

    TNB   TBW   FNB   FBW   TB   FB

13. Beavers easily make friends with other animals.

    TNB   TBW   FNB   FBW   TB   FB

14. Beavers slap their tails against the water as a warning that
    danger is near.

    TNB   TBW   FNB   FBW   TB   FB

15. Beavers spend a lot of time grooming themselves.

    TNB   TBW   FNB   FBW   TB   FB

Have you checked your answers yet? How'd you do?

Now, let's move on. Because we like you, we're going to tell
you the similarities and differences between Narnia beavers and
beavers of our world—something you probably won't learn on
the Discovery Channel or Animal Planet (at least not right now).

Here's one quick fact about beavers in both worlds: they pretty
much look the same. After all, Peter knew that Mr. Beaver was a
beaver (before Mr. Beaver admitted that fact) because of his tail.

BEAVERS IN OUR WORLD

- Do not use sewing machines
- Do not use fishing gear
- Use grass to decorate their homes
- Eat twigs and bark
- Communicate to each other

- They build dams and lodges
- They run from predators like wolves
- They store food in the winter
- They're very cautious

NARNIA BEAVERS

- Use sewing machines
- Keep fishing gear on the walls
- Have rugs, stoves, and all the comforts of a cozy English home
- Can talk to humans

Want to know more? We're just getting warmed up. Check out this handy Venn diagram. (C'mon, you've used one in school before . . . Okay, if you *really* don't know what a Venn diagram is, look at the joined circles above. A Venn diagram shows you how two things are alike and how they are different. The space between the two circles shows what the two items have in common.)

Home Sweet Home

The Beavers' lodge in *LWW* has a shape similar to those of beavers in our world—a mound about four to six feet in height above water. (Actually, Mr. and Mrs. Beavers' home is beehive-shaped, while the lodges of many beavers here look like overturned bowls, to be exact.) Mr. and Mrs. Beaver, like beavers in our world, prefer to live above the water. And like beavers in our world, Mrs. Beaver never believed that their lodge was finished. There were always repairs to be made. Yet beavers in our world may not remain in the same lodge from one season to the next. Some beavers have a winter lodge and a summer lodge.

A beaver's lodge can either be like a small island of sorts that you could get to by walking across the dam like Peter, Susan, Edmund, and Lucy did or one connected to a steep riverbank.

But that's about where the similarities between the Beavers' home and beavers' homes in our world end.

Remember how the Pevensies entered the Beavers' home (the lodge)? They walked across the top of the ice-covered dam and headed through a front door. But the lodges of beavers in our world have underwater entrances. Wondering why? Simply this—beavers have enemies. More on that later.

Although C. S. Lewis didn't go into great detail about what the Beavers' house was made of, we know that it had furniture you might find in an English country home. This fact alone shows that the Beavers of Narnia live differently from beavers in our world!

Another way they're different is through the use of tools. Mr. Beaver had building and patching tools like a trowel and a spade. Mrs. Beaver had a sewing machine. Beavers in our world don't use tools of any kind in their building or home-decorating projects. Instead, they use their paws to drag whatever they can find to the site of the dam and start building. They also use their large incisor teeth to cut down trees for use in the building.

Now, we know the big question on your mind is probably this: Could a beaver be trained to operate a sewing machine? Anything is possible to someone with loads of patience and time on his or her hands! (In other words, we're not sure.) But the question is, would a beaver *want* to use a sewing machine?

A typical beaver lodge or dam is made out of twigs, sticks, and tree saplings all laced together. A layer of mud acts like concrete and keeps predators out of the lodge.

Beavers continue adding material to their lodges and dams throughout the fall to make it cozy and safe for living in during the winter. That's why the phrase *busy as a beaver* came into being. (Lewis was as *busy as a beaver* himself in creating the Narnia series.)

Now you may wonder, *Why do beavers build dams?* Besides the fact that they have an instinct for it, beavers create an area of protection around their home by damming a pond. The dam causes the water level to rise around the lodge.

Dams are usually built evenly. Beavers add a stick here and a little bit of mud there to make the dam sturdy. Some dams are so sturdy even large animals like bears can walk across them!

Enemies at the Gate

Beavers, especially in the summer, stay on the lookout for animals like cougars, otters, lynxes, bobcats, bears, and wolves. Why? Because to these animals, beavers make a tasty snack. This is why beaver lodges have underwater entrances. When a predator (an animal higher up on the food chain than a beaver) comes, a beaver can jump into the water and hide out at home.

Like beavers in our world, Mr. and Mrs. Beaver have a wolf for an enemy. But this wolf has a name: Maugrim—one of the animals who work for the White Witch. (See chapter 11 for more on Maugrim.)

But What About Friends?

Sometimes several beaver lodges are built together and several beaver families live together in peace and friendship. But there are some friendships they would never have. It's doubtful that a beaver would invite you to his home for tea the way the Beavers invited the Pevensies. And if you noticed our list in the enemies section, you saw that beavers in our world are afraid of large felines of any kind. That's why Mr. and Mrs. Beavers' friendship with a lion named Aslan wouldn't win them any friends among beavers in our world! But Aslan was no ordinary lion. (More about him in chapter 8.)

A Day in the Life of . . .

Chapter 7 of *LWW* is all about how the Pevensies spent a day with the Beavers and began to learn what happened to Mr. Tumnus, their faun friend (think back to chapter 2). Wondering what a day in the life of a beaver from our world would be like? Here's a schedule:

8 a.m.	Sleep
9 a.m.	Sleep
10 a.m.	Sleep
11 a.m.	Sleep
3 p.m.	Eat

As you can see, in the winter, which is when *LWW* takes place, a beaver isn't very active. He or she would prefer to sleep, especially if he/she lives in a cold climate! Since many winter days are dark (most beaver lodges don't have electricity), they sleep most of the day. When they wake up, they look for food. (Does that sound like anyone you know?)

So, What do Beavers Eat?

Back in autumn, beavers would have stored food (twigs, bark) to eat during the winter. Usually, a full colony of beavers (a mom, dad, younger beavers who are one or two years old, and kits—baby beavers) would store about 1,500 pounds of food! As we told you earlier, some of the food is stored underwater as a protection against predators.

TA-DUH!

What Are Oilskins and Gumboots?

The beavers wore *oilskins* and *gumboots*. Maybe you're wondering what those are. An oilskin coat is a waterproof coat. Gumboots are rubber boots.

Sew What?

Sew, what's the story on Mrs. Beaver's sewing machine? Well, the one she used was a hand-powered model, which was considered old-fashioned even then. The earliest hand-powered sewing machines (from the nineteenth century) cranked out about twenty stitches a minute. Maybe that's why Father Christmas gave her a new sewing machine in chapter 10 of *LWW*.

As you know, a company started by Isaac Singer began manufacturing sewing machines back in the 1850s and

1860s. But he didn't invent the sewing machine. Two men—an American named Walter Hunt and a Frenchman named Barthélemy Thimonnier—are credited as the first people to create a sewing machine. But an American called Elias Howe was the first to improve on it and patent it, in 1846.

Foot-powered sewing machines were available before the 1940s. A company called Eaton's sold a model called Eatonia in 1910–50. (Perhaps Father Christmas gave Mrs. Beaver a foot-powered one!) But the Singer Company's machines were more popular.

Electric sewing machines have existed since the turn of the twentieth century. (Singer manufactured them in 1910.) But an electric sewing machine isn't very practical for someone who lives on top of a dam!

All About Mr. and Mrs. Beaver

AGE: They're not telling.

UNUSUAL CHARACTERISTICS: Mrs. Beaver wears eyeglasses; both wear snow boots.

NICKNAME(S): Mrs. Beaver calls Mr. Beaver "Mr. Beaver"; Mr. Beaver calls Mrs. Beaver "Mrs. Beaver." Other than that, they don't have nicknames. Aslan calls them "He-Beaver" and "She-Beaver."

QUALITIES: Loyal, courageous, cautious

CLAIM TO FAME: The Beavers were the first to tell the Pevensies about Aslan and prophecies about him and about them. They were quick to spot that Edmund was "treacherous."

> **LIKES/LOVES:** Mrs. Beaver loves to sew; Mr. Beaver loves to fish and eat fish.
>
> **DISLIKES:** Mrs. Beaver dislikes traitors, the White Witch, and leaving her sewing machine behind. Mr. Beaver also dislikes traitors, the White Witch, and the fact that Mrs. Beaver took forever to get ready to flee from their home.

Remember how the Narnia Beavers ate fried fish and potatoes? (Yum.) The beavers in our world are vegetarians. They also eat fruit and bark. Talk about a high-fiber diet!

So, there you have it—probably more than you ever thought you'd want to know about beavers. You don't have to thank us. It's all part of our job.

NOVICE QUIZ ANSWERS

1. D

2. B

3. B

4. C

5. B

6. A

7. D

8. A

1–3 correct   Better brush up on beavers.
4–6   Better, but still no beaver expert.

7 or more   You're a beaver behavior expert. Give yourself a pat
             on the back and a peanut butter and jelly sandwich.

INTERMEDIATE QUIZ ANSWERS

1. TB
2. FB
3. TNB
4. TB
5. TBW
6. TNB
7. TB
8. TBW
9. TBW
10. TBW
11. FB
12. TNB
13. TNB
14. TBW
15. TBW

1–5 correct   Better brush up on beavers.
6–10   Better, but still no beaver expert.
10 or more   You're a beaver behavior expert. Give yourself a pat
               on the back and a peanut butter and jelly sandwich.

CHAPTER EIGHT

We Wondered as We Wandered

No Ordinary Lion

If you read chapter 8 of *LWW*, maybe you noticed that Susan was the one who asked the most questions about Aslan. She asked questions you might have asked if you were hearing about Aslan for the first time; questions like "Who is he?" "Shall we see him?" and "Is he quite safe?" (Most lions aren't.)

Like Susan, we had questions about Aslan, questions beyond the usual "Would he eat us if we saw him?" variety. For example, *why* is he a lion? What's the deal about the prophecies concerning him? We weren't content to just wonder as we wandered through *LWW*. We did a little digging to find an answer.

WHERE *ASLAN* CAME FROM

In a letter written to a child,[1] Lewis admitted that the name Aslan was mentioned in some notes for the *Arabian Nights,* which were translated by Edward Lane. *Aslan* is the Turkish word for "lion."

---

[1] Lyle W. Dorsett and Marjorie Lamp Mead, eds., *C. S. Lewis Letters to Children* (New York: The Macmillan Company, 1985), p. 29.

First of all, an earlier draft of *LWW* didn't even have an Aslan to begin with. But after C. S. Lewis had a number of dreams about lions, he decided to put one in the story. (No, really.) Not only did he put Aslan in, he made him—well—extraordinary.

Think about all of the things you know about lions in our world, besides the physical stuff (some have manes and some don't; they're golden brown; female lions do most of the hunting; a lion's community is called a *pride*; they're good to observe from a car that has its windows tightly rolled up, etc.). Maybe you know that a lion has always been a symbol (a picture that represents something else) of power in real life and in stories. After all, he's the king of beasts. Even the Cowardly Lion of *The Wonderful Wizard of Oz* was still a ruler over beasts.

In real life, a lion is at the top of the food chain because of the animals it hunts as prey (wildebeest, zebras, impalas, gazelles, buffalo). Not Aslan. Instead of hunting other animals, he took care of them. He had to. He created them and the world they live in. (The creation of Narnia is shown in *The Magician's Nephew*.) That puts him way beyond the kind and kingly Mufasa of *The Lion King* or any other fictional lion. He can do things no ordinary lion can do (besides have a conversation with humans).

The Lion of Judah

Many people think of Aslan as Jesus in lion form. After all, Jesus was born into the family group of Judah, as the Bible describes in Matthew 1. What has that got to do with anything? Glad you asked.

The people of Israel were divided into twelve family groups, one of which was named for Jesus' ancestor, Judah. (Are you with us so far?) Thousands of years before Jesus' birth, Judah's father called Judah a lion's cub (see Genesis 49:9). (Well, being called a lion's cub is better than being called a porcupine.) Actually, Judah's father meant that Judah's family line would produce a king—the ultimate king. Jesus would be that person.

Remember that we said earlier that a lion was a symbol of power? This is one reason why Jesus is later called "the Lion of the tribe of Judah" (see Revelation 5:5). This was a way of saying that Jesus was a king.[2]

Is Aslan exactly like Jesus? In a letter to some Maryland fifth graders, written on May 29, 1954, Lewis wrote: "I did not say to myself 'Let us represent Jesus as He really is in our world by a Lion in Narnia': I said 'Let us *suppose* that there were a land like Narnia and that the Son of God, as He became a Man in our world, became a Lion there, and then imagine what would happen.'"[3]

WAYS ASLAN SEEMS LIKE JESUS

ASLAN	JESUS
• Son of the Emperor-Beyond-the-Sea	• Son of God
• Creator of the creatures of Narina	• Creator of the creatures of Earth
• Called the King of Narnia	• Called the King of kings and "the king of the Jews" (Matthew 27:37; Revelation 17:14)

[2] A thorough book on this is *The Lion in Judah in Never-Never Land* by Kathryn Ann Lindskoog (Grand Rapids, MI: William B. Eerdmans, 1973). C. S. Lewis once commented that this is one of the few books about his work that he actually liked.
[3] Dorsett and Mead, eds., *C. S. Lewis Letters to Children*, p. 44–45.

To Be an Allegory or Not to Be an Allegory: That Is the Question

Because of the similarities between Aslan and Jesus, many people believe that *LWW* is an allegory. Well, it isn't exactly. So, what exactly *is* an allegory? It's a story where the characters and story events all represent other things. A book called *Hind's Feet in High Places* by Hannah Hurnard is an allegory, because the journey of the main character (Much-Afraid) represents the Christian life. All of the characters (the Shepherd; Craven Fear; Mrs. Valiant; etc.) represent people or characteristics of people in real life.

John Bunyan's book *Pilgrim's Progress* (written back in the 1670s during a time of imprisonment) is an allegory—one of the oldest, really—for the same reason as Hurnard's book. Bunyan undoubtedly inspired Hurnard. He definitely inspired C. S. Lewis.

C. S. Lewis wrote a book called *Pilgrim's Regress* (published in 1933) as an allegory of his search for meaning in his life. But let's get back to Aslan.

Facts About the Future

Remember how Mr. Beaver talked about spring as a sign of Aslan's return? He quoted what he called "an old rhyme" and later called it a "prophecy." What's a prophecy? It's a prediction of a future event. As the Pevensies learned, there were a number of prophecies about Aslan and one specifically about them.

Some people look at prophecies like a fortune cookie—a statement made for entertainment purposes that either won't happen, or is so general it could happen for anyone. (For example, "You will find happiness.") But a prophecy is considered more than just a prediction. It is an event that is believed to be true *before it happens*.

Prophecies are pretty specific. For example, the Bible mentions several prophecies about a Savior to come. These prophecies were spoken hundreds of years before the birth of the Savior. They explain where he would be born (Micah 5:2, a book toward the end of the Old Testament, mentions the town—Bethlehem) and what would happen to him (he would suffer during his life—Isaiah 53). Jesus is believed to be the one who fulfilled those prophecies (made them come true, in other words).

Many fairy tales feature prophecies of some kind. In a Russian folktale called "Bearskin," retold by Howard Pyle in his book *The Wonder Clock,* an evil king, after hearing a prophecy about a boy who will grow up to marry his daughter and become king, tries to kill the child before the prophecy can come true. The White Witch tries to do the same thing in *LWW*.

The White Witch's reaction to the prophecy also is similar to that of Herod in the real-life story of Jesus. Maybe you've sung the Christmas carol "We Three Kings." The song is all about the wise men (Magi) who followed a star to find the newly born king. Having studied the stars, they found a new one, which for them meant that a king had been born. After Herod, the king of the nation of Israel, talked to the wise men, he ordered his men to kill all boys two years old and under to prevent anyone from growing up and taking over his throne. (See Matthew 2. Unfortunately, even this terrible event was a prophecy fulfilled. That prophecy can be found in Jeremiah 31:15.) But what Herod and the White Witch didn't realize was that prophecies have a way of coming true. If you read the rest of *LWW,* you'll know they did.

Not Safe? What Does That Mean?

There are some other characteristics of Aslan (besides the prophecies) that really stuck out in our minds. Remember back in chapter 7 of *LWW* when the Beavers mentioned that Aslan wasn't safe? We wondered what that meant exactly. Oh, we know why lions in our world aren't safe. Lions may look cute and cuddly, but they're fierce predators with sharp teeth and claws. (See our little "lion," p. 219.) Their forepaws are extremely powerful. No one who knows the real nature of lions would walk up to one in the wild and try to pet him or her. If one wanted to charge you, you would have about six seconds to escape.

Beyond the fact that Aslan has sharp teeth and even sharper claws, his lack of safety shows his nature: he's not tame or predictable. This doesn't mean he's uncivilized. After all, he's the true King of Narnia! He balances kindness with justice. He allows kids to hug him (see chapter 15 of *LWW*), but he's fierce in a fight against enemies (chapter 16).

According to many stories in the Bible, this is God's nature. He's good, but not safe or predictable.

Awe of Aslan

In chapter 12 of *LWW,* when the Pevensies actually meet Aslan, they decide that a thing *can* be "good and terrible" at the same time. Ever look at the sky or look down from a great height and suddenly feel small? Then you know how the Pevensies felt about Aslan.

By terrible, Lewis doesn't mean *disgusting*. He means that Aslan can't be controlled or contained. In other words, he's powerful. We might say that a storm is *terrible,* because it has the power to cause great destruction.

The Pevensies could sense something different about Aslan. He wasn't a creature they could take lightly. He was too powerful for that.

Lewis believed these things about God—that He was both good and terrible. This feeling also is known as *awe*. Not *aw* as in "Aww, how cute," but *awe* as in "I'm in the presence of someone or something amazing, something waaaayyyy bigger than me, something I don't quite understand, which scares me."

As you know, there are two kinds of fear: terror in which one feels dread, and fear in the presence of something way bigger and more powerful than yourself. (No, not like someone older or a bully or something.) This is a nervous kind of feeling about ten times greater than if you met the president or saw an ancient building that stood on the same spot for thousands of years.

All About Aslan

AGE: He's ageless.

NARNIA TITLE(S): The King; Lord of the whole wood; Son of the great Emperor-beyond-the-Sea; the great Lion; *the* Lion; the true King; the King of Beasts

QUALITIES: He's far bigger than a normal lion. He's not safe or tame, but he's good. He's concerned about truth and justice. He has "terrible" but thankfully "velveted" paws, and "unchanging eyes" that also are "royal, solemn, and overwhelming."

CLAIM TO FAME: He's the one who died for Edmund. He's also the creator of Narnia and the one who came back to life after dying. His return to Narnia brings spring and ends the witch's winter chill over Narnia. Best of all, he's the one who defeats the White Witch.

LIKES/LOVES: All people and beasts. He likes to romp like a kitten.

SOUNDS HE'S KNOWN FOR: Roaring; purring

DISLIKES: He is against anything the witch stands for (evil, for one thing). He doesn't like lying or when animals and people don't believe in him.

SAYINGS ABOUT: "Aslan is on the move"; "in the name of Aslan" (which means, "by his authority"); "by the Lion's Mane"

The Stone Age

Aside from talking about Aslan (and who wouldn't want to do that?), remember how the Beavers talked about the animals that were turned to stone by the White Witch? (She could never turn Aslan to stone.) She's not the only fairy-tale person to turn someone into stone. There are many stories where people or objects are turned to stone or are petrified in some way. You may know about the basilisk—that huge snake that petrified people in *Harry Potter and the Chamber of Secrets*. But C. S. Lewis would have known the following stories:

MEDUSA One of the most well known stories is about Medusa from Greek mythology. As we mentioned in chapter 5b, C. S. Lewis studied the classics, which included Greek myths. Know anything about Medusa? Medusa had snakes for hair. (Talk about a bad hair day—she had bad hair *years*.) One glance at her turned a person to stone. You see, Medusa was a gorgon—a female monster. She used to be a normal woman, blessed with beauty, but was punished by Athena, the Greek goddess of war, wisdom, and the arts. (That's a long story.) She had two sisters who also had the same unusual hair.

One day, a guy named Perseus was challenged by King Polydectes (a name that's a mouthful) to kill Medusa. In order to avoid looking directly at Medusa, Perseus looked at the reflection in his shield as he crept up to Medusa to carry out his mission. Not a pretty story.

ARABIAN NIGHTS Ever read the *Arabian Nights* (edited by Andrew Lang, but originally translated by Edward William Lane from *1001 Arabian Nights*)? (FYI: C. S. Lewis admitted that he was not a big fan of the *Arabian Nights* stories. He did, however, like some of Andrew Lang's other story collections.) This is a collection of stories told by Scheherezade, the daughter of the grand vizier to a sultan. (A grand vizier was like a prime minister.) Scheherezade told about 1001 stories—one story each day—to keep herself alive. (Another long story.) In one of those stories, "The Story of the Young King of the Black Isles," a king was partially turned into stone by an evil sorceress.

THE PINK FAIRY BOOK In "The Water of Life," a story from *The Pink Fairy Book,* edited by Andrew Lang (yeah, he was kinda busy back in the nineteenth century), three brothers go on a quest for—you guessed it—the water of life. But this quest came with a unique set of directions. All of the brothers ignored one of the directions and instantly were turned into a stone. Their sister had to complete the quest for them. (What else is a sister to do?)

THE BIBLE In a story in the Bible (Genesis 19), two angels warned a man named Lot (the nephew of Abraham) that his city (Sodom) would be destroyed. Before that happened, the angels told Lot and his family to run away and not look back. Lot's wife disobeyed that command and was turned to a pillar of salt when she looked back at the destruction of Sodom.

LILITH WHO?

Mr. Beaver told the Pevensies that Lilith was Adam's first wife. You might wonder, *Is that true? Did Adam really have a wife besides Eve?* There is no one in the Bible named Lilith. There is a story in an ancient book called *The Alphabet of Ben-Sira,* which is a collection of stories from the Bible and the Talmud (an ancient collection of Jewish laws and writings by rabbis). But the story of Lilith, a supposedly evil woman, has generally been considered a myth—something not true. C. S. Lewis mentioned Lilith to explain the evil origin of Jadis—the White Witch. She's definitely not human.

Mr. Beaver also said that Lilith was one of the Jinn (aka Djinn). In many stories, the Jinn are spirits who have the

---

power to grant wishes. They can be completely evil (as in the case of Lilith) or good (like the Genie in Disney's *Aladdin*). There are many stories of Jinn in the *Arabian Nights* (where the story of Aladdin comes from). In many of the stories, Jinn are troublesome spirits who make the lives of humans miserable.

CHAPTER NINE

Into the Dark Side

A Boy Behaving Badly

Ever do something you knew would lead to trouble? We all have. At some point we have a chance of turning back. But sometimes, we go ahead, thinking, *Might as well keep going. It's too late to turn back now.*

Take Edmund, for instance. Tsk, tsk. Oh, he was very naughty in *LWW*, very naughty indeed, especially in chapter 9, when he decided to head to the witch's house. Not cool at all. Like Anakin Skywalker in the *Star Wars* movies, Edmund was about to cross over into the dark side. But he's not the only one to behave badly. In fact, Edmund's story resembles that of some others we know.

STORY 1: A SECRET MEETING

Picture if you will the sun-baked streets of Jerusalem during the first century. (Okay, maybe you can't picture them if you haven't been there. Just play along.) Watch as a man slips off for a secret meeting with the leaders of his people. He agrees to lead them to his friend and teacher—a man he just left—for a price: 30 pieces of silver. (Edmund's price was lots more Turkish Delight.)

Maybe this man, like Edmund, fools himself into thinking that his friend wouldn't suffer any permanent harm. Perhaps, he thinks, the leaders only want to question his friend or make him pay a fine.

But they didn't want to just question his friend. They wanted him as dead as the White Witch wanted Edmund's siblings. (More on that in chapter 13.) They were jealous of the success of his friend, who was a very popular teacher and miracleworker. But they needed someone close to this man to lead him into a trap. That way, all the blame for his arrest would fall on the person who betrayed him.

Who was this man? He was Judas, the man who betrayed Jesus (see Luke 22—a chapter of a book in the New Testament; unlike Edmund, Judas was a real person in history). Because of his betrayal, his name became a synonym for *traitor*. Maybe that's why the name "Judas" is not a popular baby name nowadays.

The funny thing was that Jesus knew that Judas would betray him. While eating a special meal (Passover) with his followers, he suddenly announced: "Truly I say to you that one of you will betray Me—one who is eating with Me" (Mark 14:18, *New American Standard Bible*). He then said, "Woe to the man by whom the Son of Man is betrayed! It would have been good for that man if he had not been born" (verse 21). He was right.

Remember when the Beavers determined that Edmund would betray them? While eating with him, they had a feeling that he was up to no good. Obviously, they were right.

C. S. Lewis knew all about the story of Judas' betrayal. While writing *LWW*, he didn't set out to copy that story. Yet certain parts of the story of Jesus "fit themselves" into the story. In an essay (he wrote a lot of those) called "Sometimes Fairy Stories May Say Best What's to Be Said," he noted, "At first there wasn't even anything Christian about [the images he saw in his head—the faun, the White Witch]; that element pushed itself in of its own accord."[1]

---

[1] *On Stories and Other Essays on Literature*, p. 46.

STORY 2: A COLD PLACE

As we followed Edmund's cold, dark journey to the witch's house, we thought of another story: "The Snow Queen," written by Hans Christian Andersen in 1846. Ever read it? Then you know all about Kai, a normally nice boy who didn't realize that small pieces of glass from an evil mirror had landed in his eye and heart. These shards changed his personality, making him cold and mean even to his best friend, Gerda. The Snow Queen, a creature he didn't believe existed, later carried him off to her palace. Because his heart was frozen, he felt right at home there.

Check out these comparisons. Weird, huh?

WHITE WITCH	SNOW QUEEN
• Calls herself the queen of her land	• Is called the queen of her land
• Drives a sledge	• Drives a sled
• Tricks a boy into running away to her castle	• Carries a boy away to live in her palace
• Is tall and has a chalk-white face	• Is tall and made of snow
• Acts sweet at first, then becomes mean	• So "kind" to Kai that he almost freezes to death from her kisses

The Snow Queen is cold, but not as menacing as the White Witch, who seems to be pure evil. If you were to meet either one of them, run.

Because he can't help himself, Kai has to be rescued by Gerda. Sounds a lot like what happens to Edmund later in *LWW*, right?

Home Dank Home

There is a moment in many stories (real life or fictional) where a character is forced to enter the house, castle, or secret lair of the villain of the story. Usually that's part of the *rising action* of a story. What do we mean? We mean the chain of events that lead to the *climax* of a story—the point of greatest tension. You can feel your heart race and your adrenaline kick in as a hero or heroine takes a step toward what could be his or her doom.

Sometimes the hero or heroine approaches the villain's creepy lair at the climax of the story. But Edmund's journey to the witch's house is part of the rising action of *LWW*. His betrayal sets other events in motion—events that bring about the climax of *LWW*. (When the Pevensies first discovered Narnia, the rising action began.)

But there are other journeys characters have made toward the lair of the villain. Think of the three good fairies (Flora, Fauna, and Merryweather) who travel to the castle of Maleficent, the evil fairy in *Sleeping Beauty* (the Disney movie version). Or how about Dorothy and the Cowardly Lion, who are captured by the flying monkeys and dragged off to the castle of the Wicked Witch of the West in *The Wonderful Wizard of Oz*? And let's not forget Gerda, who travels all the way to Lapland (an area in Northern Europe that crosses Norway, Finland, Sweden, and part of Russia) to rescue Kai from the castle of the Snow Queen.

Usually, the villain's lair is about as dark and dank as your imagination can make it (unless you're watching a movie that basically shows you how it looks).

Out of the three stories described above, only the Wicked Witch of the West seems to have any decorating skills. L. Frank Baum, the author of *Oz*, describes her rooms as "beautiful." But the homes of the White Witch, Maleficent, and the Snow Queen seem to give new meaning to the phrase *dark and dank*. Check out their domains:

WHITE WITCH	SNOW QUEEN	MALEFICENT
She lives in a small stone castle with towers with cruel-looking pointed spires. Animals that have been turned to stone decorate the courtyard. The house also has a fierce wolf for a "welcome mat." Everything you need to feel right at home.	Her home is described as "empty, vast, and cold." It even has a frozen lake inside. It contains hundreds of rooms and has walls made of snow with windows and doors made of winds. (At least her heating bill is low.)	In her decorating, she seems to live by the C's: crumbling stone, cobwebs, and cruel creatures to guard her castle. She can't call Martha Stewart fast enough.

A Dark Time for C. S. Lewis

In *LWW*, C. S. Lewis mentioned that Edmund started to go wrong at school. He could relate to what Edmund went through.

In chapter 5a, we told you that Lewis went to a prep school—a boarding school—at Malvern. Before he went there, he went to a school called Wynyard soon after his mother died. He hated that school, because of the severe punishments of the harsh headmaster (a man he called "Oldie").

He was thirteen when he went to Cherbourg (the prep school at Malvern) and was determined to put aside religion.

He hung out with his friends and took up smoking. (He still managed to make good grades in school, however.) But after that, he went to Malvern College—the same school his brother Warren attended. Although he made some good friends, he grew to hate the school, because of the school hierarchy.

What was the school hierarchy? Every school has one, which comes with its own set of labels. You know: the popular kids, the outcasts, the in-betweens, the jocks—the list goes on.

At Malvern, the popular kids were the bloods—the "school aristocracy," as Lewis mentions in *Surprised by Joy*. The bloods had the unofficial right to order younger boys to do what they wanted (cleaning their shoes, for instance). The bloods knew that the younger students sought their friendship in order to have status. So, they mistreated them, because they could.

Lewis was tired of the constant phoniness of the system. Yet, as an adult looking back at the experience, he realized that his personality was changing at the time. He had become the person he disliked: a *prig* (a word Edmund uses in chapter 6, which means someone phony and conceited).

TA-DUH!

How a Modern Road Is Made

While on his way to the witch's house, Edmund decided that if he were king, he would get some decent roads made. Wondering how a road is made? Well, the first thing road planners do is decide where it should go. (Through your neighbor's house or your brother's bedroom? No good.) They usually estimate the amount of traffic that will go on the road. They have to determine whether or not the site chosen will support the weight of the cars or trucks that will travel on it year after year. How will the new road affect the traffic on other roads?

Construction begins after the planning stage and after the planners know how the road will be paid for (usually by taxes). Surveyors come in to mark the boundaries of the road. Workers then set to work building the drainage system for the road. The soil is checked, before it is flattened to form the bottom layer of the road. All plants (weeds, etc.) are removed.

The next stage is to add asphalt (if the pavement is to be flexible) or concrete (if the pavement is to be rigid) with the use of a paving machine. (Road planners determine whether a road is flexible or rigid beforehand.) Asphalt expands or contracts, depending on the weather. It sends moisture off the road toward the sides. Concrete, on the other hand, shrinks and cracks as it hardens. But cracking is controlled by the addition of steel reinforcement.

A top layer of hot bitumen (which comes from liquid petroleum) is sprayed over the road. Stone chips are blended with the bitumen. Together, they make a spray-and-chip seal. The excess stones are cleared away later.

Dwarfs(ves) in Mythology

Okay. Let's clear something up first. Is *dwarves* or *dwarfs* correct? The answer is both are used in stories. But since Tolkien used *dwarves* in *Lord of the Rings,* a lot of people use *dwarves.* (Isn't your life richer for knowing that? C'mon, humor us.)

A number of dwarves work for a witch. What stories come to mind when you think of dwarves? *Lord of the Rings!* "Rumplestiltskin," by the brothers Grimm? Disney's *Snow White and the Seven Dwarfs!* Dwarves pop up a lot in fairy stories. They come from Norse myths. In those stories, dwarves live in a place called Nidavellir. (Well, you didn't expect them to live in Scranton or Little Rock, did you?)

We've said enough times that C. S. Lewis read and loved Norse myths. He had that in common with his friend Arthur Greeves. As a teen, he even composed an opera about some of the gods of Norse mythology.[2]

Like Tolkien, Lewis used dwarves in his stories. You can find red-haired and black-haired dwarves in the Narnia stories. In chapter 2 of *LWW,* Mr. Tumnus tells Lucy about "wild" red dwarves. (Both are mentioned in *Prince Caspian.*) The red-haired dwarves seemed loyal to Aslan, while the black-haired dwarves sided with the witch.

Whether they're called "hill men" (by the Swiss) or *Kropel* (by the Germans), dwarves have similar characteristics in most myths.

Dwarves are described as shorter in height than men— usually about three feet tall. (The White Witch's sidekick is about three feet high; Tolkien's dwarves look a little bigger.) They live in mountains and are skilled at mining and smithing (creating beautiful things out of silver, gold, and

[2] See Terry Lindvall, *Surprised by Laughter: The Comic World of C. S. Lewis* (Nashville, TN: Thomas Nelson, 1996), p. 85.

other metals). (Think of the occupation of the Seven Dwarves in *Snow White*.) They're also known to have long beards.

They live a lot longer than people. In stories, they live for hundreds of years.

DWARVES IN OTHER STORIES

- *The Blue Fairy Book,* Andrew Lang's collection of fairy tales, has a number of stories featuring dwarves. These include "The Yellow Dwarf" (an evil dwarf tries to gain a wife); "The Sleeping Beauty in the Woods" (yes, it is a Sleeping Beauty story, featuring only one dwarf, not seven); "The White Cat" (evil dwarves are run out of a kingdom); "Snow White and Rose Red" (more evil dwarves).

- Sindri and Brokk—two dwarves in Norse myths. Sindri and Brokk are brothers who made a ring of power which Odin (the god of wisdom and war) used.

- Gimli son of Glóin in *Lord of the Rings*—he is one of the nine companions in the first book of Tolkien's trilogy.

- In *The Hobbit* by Tolkien, Bilbo accompanies thirteen dwarves on a treasure hunt.

All About Edmund

AGE: He might be ten. He's older than Lucy, but younger than Susan.

BIRTH ORDER: The third of the Pevensie children

NICKNAME(S): Ed (family nickname); "poisonous little beast" (Peter calls him that in anger); the little Prince (the dwarf who worked for the White Witch calls him that sarcastically); "the brat" (the White Witch calls him that)

QUALITIES: At times, he can be spiteful and selfish; he tries to compete with Peter. Friends at his school possibly led him astray. When he grows up in Narnia, he becomes a grave, quiet man, with good judgment.

CLAIM TO FAME: He's the one who betrays his siblings, which causes Aslan to have to die for him. After he is forgiven, he is later knighted after the battle with the White Witch and her army.

LIKES/LOVES: Turkish Delight; teasing Lucy. Like Peter (see chapter 12 of this book), he would've liked pulling apart the armor in the Professor's house if he had the chance.

DISLIKES: Admitting when he's wrong; being alone in strange places

GIFT FROM FATHER CHRISTMAS: He's the only Pevensie who didn't receive one. (See, that's what happens when you betray people: you get put on the "naughty" list.)

NARNIA TITLE(S): King Edmund; Edmund the Just; Son of Adam

CHAPTER TEN

𝔍 𝔓lace for 𝔍ather 𝔒hristmas

𝔥o-𝔥o 𝔫o 𝔫o?

Christmastime. For those of you who celebrate the holiday, is there a more delightful time of year (besides your birthday and summer vacation)? Think about the best Christmas you ever had. What made it the best?

Most of us, if we're honest, would say that the gifts we get can make or break Christmas. Maybe you can recall some good and some awful gifts you received. We certainly can. It's funny how the awful gifts stay in your mind longer than the really good ones. Like that awful sweater your aunt Petunia knitted you that's not only the wrong color, but from the wrong era—something more appropriate for a display in a museum. Yikes.

Imagine being in a place where Christmas was never celebrated. But that was the state of Narnia when the Pevensies arrived. What would you do if there were no Christmas to look forward to in the middle of winter? Just think of how Christmas makes a nice break in the winter and provides relief from winter blahs.

For many people (and certainly for the animals and other creatures of Narnia), Christmas is made jolly because of Santa Claus, or Father Christmas as he's called in the United Kingdom. Yet he's the one addition to Narnia that Lewis's friends, J. R. R. Tolkien and

Roger Lancelyn Green (see chapter 5b), disagreed with him the most about.

What did they have against Father Christmas? Nothing—they simply didn't believe he belonged in Narnia! But as you can see for yourself if you read chapter 10 of *LWW,* Father Christmas remains in the story.

Ironically, a book of Father Christmas letters to Tolkien's children recently was re-released (*Letters from Father Christmas* by J. R. R. Tolkien, published by HarperCollins & Houghton Mifflin). The book shows twenty years' worth of letters containing stories about Father Christmas, his elf secretary, and a battle with goblins.

Have a Holly Jolly Christmas?

By now, you're probably wondering why C. S. Lewis insisted on having Father Christmas in the story. We wondered that as well, especially after seeing a childhood picture of Lewis with a Father Christmas doll.

The fact is, we don't know exactly how Lewis felt about Father Christmas. But he did make clear that Aslan was the most important being in Narnia. After all, in chapter 10 of *LWW,* Father Christmas declares, "Long live the true King!" and seems to have an authority given to him by Aslan.

What we do know is how Lewis felt about Christmas. Although he enjoyed the holiday (except for one miserable Christmas back in 1922 when he was a teen; maybe you can recall a disappointing one yourself), there were some things he didn't like about it.

Ever watch the Charlie Brown Christmas special? They've shown it on TV for about forty years. Anyway, remember how Charlie Brown complained about the commercialization of Christmas? C. S. Lewis had the same complaint. In an essay called

"What Christmas Means to Me,"[1] written in 1957, Lewis wrote about "the commercial racket" of Christmas. He was sad that the pressure to buy and give gifts crowded out the celebration of the birth of Christ (he also mentioned this in letters to people over the years). For Lewis, holiday stress was more of an Xmas or "Exmas" thing.

You read it right: Exmas. Three years before that (1954), Lewis wrote a story called "Xmas and Christmas: A Lost Chapter from Herodotus." Okay, that might all seem like Greek to you, but it showed what C. S. Lewis thought about the ways that Christmas has been commercialized. The story describes a mythical place called Niatirb (Britain spelled backward), where Exmas was celebrated instead of Christmas. The people of this land raced around buying things for others during the "Exmas Rush." Does that sound familiar?

A few people in Niatirb celebrate a holiday called "Crissmas." Gift giving is not the most important thing about this holiday. Celebrating the birth of a child is. (And we think we all know the identity of that child.) But the celebration of Exmas distracted the other people from celebrating Crissmas.

After C. S. Lewis started believing in the God of the Bible once more, he saw Christmas as a time to celebrate the birth of Christ. Does this mean he was a "Scrooge" who didn't like Christmas cheer? No. As he said in "What Christmas Means to Me," "I should say that I much approve of merry-making." He was a man who loved to laugh and hang out with friends.

With *LWW*, he celebrates the return of Aslan—something even Father Christmas looked forward to. When readers asked him about Aslan and Father Christmas, Lewis suggested that they remember that Father Christmas didn't come until Aslan returned.

---

[1] This essay appears in a book of essays by Lewis entitled *God in the Dock* (Grand Rapids, MI: William B. Eerdmans, 1970).

Father Christmas and Santa

Now, American readers might wonder what differences, if any, there are between Father Christmas and the Santa we're used to. Traditionally, Father Christmas has worn a long red robe with a hood trimmed in fur. Santa, as you know, wears a red suit, but no hood.

Lewis's Father Christmas is a little different from the Father Christmas of our world. He works for Aslan and is a subject of Aslan's kingdom. That means he knows that Aslan is in charge. What's also different is the fact that he comes in the spring. Usually, he comes on Christmas Eve!

Also, the Father Christmas in Narnia speaks with authority. He tells Susan and Lucy that he doesn't mean for them to fight in the battle. Father Christmas doesn't usually tell people what to do except "Be good or you'll be put on the naughty list."

Although Lewis's Father Christmas gives gifts like the Father Christmas in our world, these gifts are a little bit different, too. How different? We'll tell you.

Armed for Battle

As far as Christmas gifts are concerned, would you rather have something you wanted or something you needed?

Remember the gifts Father Christmas gave the Pevensies? He didn't give the usual Christmas gifts of that era (dolls, trains, or other toys, sweaters, etc). He gave gifts they needed, not what they wanted. Peter received a sword and shield; Susan received a bow, a quiver of arrows, and a horn. Lucy received a vial with a healing cordial.

What do you think would've happened if Lucy received a doll

or an Xbox game (not that those were around back then)? She wouldn't have been prepared for the battle ahead.

These gifts were in no way "commercial"—something C. S. Lewis disliked. They were practical, offering protection against enemies and illness.

The gifts from Father Christmas to Peter remind us of another set of gifts—gifts that also offer protection. In a Bible book called Ephesians (which is really a letter, but we're not getting into that right now), there is a chapter on spiritual armor (Ephesians 6:10–17). This isn't the kind of armor C. S. Lewis mentions in chapter 5 of *LWW*. The kind of armor a man named Paul wrote about is spiritual or symbolic. We can't see it, but it's there. It's used to fight enemies like temptation or fear. Paul mentions a "shield of faith" (verse 16) and "the sword of the Spirit" (verse 17). Faith is belief in something you can't see. The sword of the Spirit is the Bible and a person's knowledge of it.

Lewis believed in the God of the Bible who is three in one: a trinity (God, Son, Holy Spirit). In a way, Father Christmas is like the Holy Spirit, the one who provides spiritual armor and the power to use it.

The Gift of a Sword

Speaking of powerful gifts, someone else in a fairy tale (besides Peter) was given a sword. Think of the most famous sword in fiction (other than Sting or Glamdring of Tolkien's books). We're thinking about Excalibur. The hand that wielded it was King Arthur's.

Grammar note: To *wield* a sword means "to handle a weapon with skill and ease," according to the *American Heritage College Dictionary*. So, you wouldn't say, "She amazed everyone with the way she *wielded* a marshmallow," because that would be silly. Now, you could say, "The blue pillow was mine to wield in our pillow fight," because (a) the pillow is a weapon in a battle and (b) we said you could. But we're getting away from our story.

You probably know the story of King Arthur. C. S. Lewis certainly did. As a kid he read Mark Twain's *A Connecticut Yankee in King Arthur's Court*. But when he grew up, he read *Le Morte d'Arthur* by Thomas Malory (published in 1485). This is the ultimate story of King Arthur—the book that inspired many fantasy writers, including T. H. White, who wrote *The Once and Future King* (his version of the story of King Arthur).

If you saw the Disney movie *The Sword in the Stone* or read White's book, you know that young Arthur (Wart) pulled a sword out of an anvil in a churchyard while a tournament took place. This action proclaimed him as the true King of England. (And he really was the true king, being the son of Uther Pendragon, the last king.)

This sword, however, was not Excalibur. You see, the sword Arthur pulled from the stone was broken during a fight with the Black Knight. (That's a long story.) Because he needed a sword, Merlin took him to the Lady of the Lake—a fairy. She agreed to give Arthur Excalibur, the greatest sword in the world. But he had to promise to return it to her.

Yet, as powerful as that sword was, the scabbard (the case used to house a sword) was more powerful. Having the scabbard would keep Arthur from being killed in a battle.

Christmas in Great Britain

Perhaps after seeing Father Christmas in action in chapter 10 of *LWW* or the animals and satyrs throwing a Christmas party (chapter 11), or after your hundredth time of seeing the movie version of Dickens's *A Christmas Carol,* you felt curious about how Christmas is celebrated in England. (Or perhaps you already know a lot about Christmas in England and just want to review.)[2]

Many of the traditions practiced in Great Britain today got

[2] A great book on English Christmas traditions is Celia McInnes, *An English Christmas* (New York: Henry Holt & Co., 1986).

their start during the Victorian era (the years of the reign of Queen Victoria: 1837–1901). Charles Dickens wrote his classic tale of Christmas during that time. Christmas trees, a tradition started by the Germans, have been a tradition in England since Prince Albert (husband of Queen Victoria) brought one to Windsor Castle in 1841.

Kids in England write letters to Father Christmas just like kids write to Santa here in the States. Years ago, the letters were thrown into the fireplace instead of being posted. (Father Christmas, you see, could read the smoke.) Nowadays, most of the letters are mailed.

Caroling is a popular pastime that dates back to the Middle Ages. In fact, caroling became a tradition here in the States because of the English tradition.

For decorations, holly, ivy, and other greenery (mistletoe, for instance) are hung. Traditionally, hanging greenery was a way to add cheer to the winter blahs. (A nice mug of hot chocolate has the same effect for us.)

CHRISTMAS EVE On Christmas Eve, a Yule log is placed on the fire (for those who have fireplaces and like to observe the old traditions). The log is supposed to be lit with a piece from the previous year's log. Stockings are hung up by the chimney. (We do that in America, because of the tradition started in England.) A mince pie is left out for Father Christmas. (We leave milk and cookies here in the U.S.)

Plays known as mummers' plays (plays where performers wear masks and perform using pantomime) used to be performed on Christmas Eve. Sometimes a play about St. George was performed. (You'll find out more about St. George in chapter 12.)

CHRISTMAS DAY On Christmas Day, foods like roast goose or turkey, mince pies, and plum pudding are served. A hot drink called wassail has traditionally been served. It's made of mulled ale or cider, apples, spices, nuts, eggs, and curdled cream. The word *wassail* comes from an Anglo Saxon phrase *waes hael*, meaning "Good health."

Also, what's a Christmas without crackers? These aren't the salted kind; these are treats (paper hats, small toys, and gifts) inserted in a tube wrapped in brightly colored paper, which is then tied at two ends. When you and another person each pull at opposite ends, you hear a cracking sound as the paper pulls apart. Maybe you've tried one! (A baker named Thomas Smith invented them during the nineteenth century.)

During the afternoon, the queen broadcasts a Christmas message just as the president takes time on Christmas Day to send his greetings here.

CHRISTMAS: THE EXTENDED VERSION In Great Britain, Christmas extends beyond just December 25. Boxing Day and the Feast of St. Stephen are celebrated on December 26. (Stephen was the first person to die for his Christian beliefs. You can find his story in Acts 6–7 of the Bible.) Boxing Day is a day to remember the poor. Gifts are given to faithful workers and to the less fortunate.

This day marks the beginning of the Twelve Days of Christmas (December 26 to January 6, a day known as Epiphany)—a tradition since the sixth century. (Now the Christmas carol "The Twelve Days of Christmas" makes sense, huh? Unless you're still wondering about the partridge in the pear tree.) New Year's Day provides another opportunity to light the Yule log.

A dried bean is hidden in a cake known as a Twelfth Night cake, which is eaten on January 6. The person who finds the bean is the king or queen for the whole day. (Good deal!)

ANSWERS TO FATHER CHRISTMAS BY ANY OTHER NAME QUIZ

1. Santa Claus (United States)

2. Père Nöel (France)

3. Babbo Natale (Italy)

4. Grandfather Frost (Russia)

5. Sinte Klaas (The Netherlands)

6. St. Nikolaus/Kris Kringle/ Der Weinachtsmann (Germany)

7. Niklaus/Christkindl (Austria)

CHAPTER ELEVEN

The Fast and the Furious (and We're Not Crying Wolf)

Hungry Like the Wolf?

Think about the wolves you've read about in fairy tales (or seen in movies based on fairy tales). Maybe you know about

- the "Big Bad Wolf" of "The Three Little Pigs."

- the Wolf in "Little Red Riding Hood" who gobbled up Red (the Andrew Lang version).

- Aesop's fables, which feature many stories of wolves and their craving for sheep (like "The Wolf and the Lamb," "The Wolf in Sheep's Clothing," "The Wolves and the Sheep," "The Shepherd's Boy and the Wolf"— better known as "The Boy who Cried wolf," "The Shepherd and the Wolf," "The Wolf and the Sheep"— the list goes on).

- fairy tales by the brothers Grimm like "The Wolf and the Seven Little Kids" (this time, the Wolf wanted to gobble goats), "The Wolf and the Fox" (a hungry, cruel wolf is tricked by a wily fox), and others, including a version of

"Little Red Riding Hood." (The grandmother foils the hungry Wolf this time.)

- the wolves who run alongside the train in *The Polar Express* (the book and movie) (at least they're not gobbling sheep).

What do you notice? Mostly cunning, angry wolves out for prey. Stories like the ones above and an old Duran Duran song called "Hungry Like the Wolf" show what people have thought of wolves over the centuries—as the fast and the furious. (In other words, negatively.)

Who's Afraid of the Big Bad Wolf?

In chapter 11 of *LWW,* we meet another cunning wolf: Maugrim (actually, we first meet him in chapter 9). Now, you might wonder, *Why did C. S. Lewis make Maugrim evil? What does he have against wolves?* The answer is, probably nothing. This is a fairy tale, ol' chap. (You don't mind if we call you that, do you? Since you've been with us for eleven chapters now, we feel really close to you.) Maugrim is probably an *archetype*. What's an archetype? "An ancient pattern of personality," according to Christopher Vogler in his book *The Writer's Journey: Mythic Structure for Writers*.[1]

What did he mean by that? Well, in many fairy tales, you see the same kinds of characters over and over (heroes and heroines on quests; wise leaders; villains). We've already talked about how many fairy tales have wolves with similar characteristics (hungry; angry; after sheep or other prey). Wondering why? Because writers long ago established the pattern.

[1] This definition came from Carl Jung, a psychologist. We just thought you'd want to know that. Vogler's book was published by Michael Wiese Productions (Studio City, CA) in 1998.

Aesop, a former slave turned writer who lived about 600 B.C., was one of the earliest writers to write about sly, hungry wolves. Whether or not he observed real wolves in the wild is anybody's guess.

The wolf has a rather negative image even in the Bible. In the Gospel of John (the fourth book in the New Testament), Jesus promises to protect his flock (those who follow his commandments) as a shepherd would protect his flock against an attacking wolf (John 10:12).

Norse myths (stories from the Viking era, A.D. 800–1100) are another group of stories partially responsible for the negative view of wolves. Loki, an evil god in these myths (there's always an evil one), had a man-eating wolf (Fenrir) for a son! (C. S. Lewis was fond of Norse myths. Perhaps that's why Maugrim's name in the British version of *LWW* is Fenris Ulf.) Because of these stories, many people believed that wolves were evil.

During the seventeenth to the nineteenth centuries, people in Europe passed around stories of man-eating wolves, which added to the hearsay about wolves.[2]

So, What's the Real Story?

Are wolves really evil man-eaters? No. Wolf attacks on humans have been extremely rare. Usually, a wolf will only attack in self-defense. But many people have the attitude that wolves attack like Maugrim does in chapter 12 of *LWW*.

There *has* been an ongoing battle between humans and wolves for thousands of years, however. As people established farms and took over more of the wilderness, they also hunted deer and other

---

[2] One great book on wolves is *Trail of the Wolf* by R. D. Lawrence (New York: Firefly Books, 1993, 1997). Another is Robert H. Busch, *The Wolf Almanac* (New York: The Lyons Press, 1995, 1998).

animals for food—animals that wolves hunted too. So, the wolves had to find other food. Like any predator (lions, cheetahs, crocodiles, etc.), wolves followed their instincts. They considered animals on farms or ranches fair game. (They aren't acquainted with laws concerning trespassing or stealing.)

So, people grew to hate wolves and passed around stories about evil ones. The offer of bounties by private citizens and the government encouraged hunters to kill wolves. As a result of that and the value placed on their fur, many hunters hunted wolves nearly to extinction.

Within the last century, wildlife organizations and groups like the International Union for the Conservation of Nature and Natural Resources have put a stop to the wholesale killing of wolves. In 1973, the gray wolf was placed on the endangered species list.

TA-DUH!

Wolf Types

Okay, you know that Maugrim was a gray wolf. And maybe you know that wolves and dogs belong to the same larger family group (*Canidae*). Did you know that there are three species of wolves? Yep, the gray wolf, the red wolf, and the Abyssinian wolf (aka the Ethiopian wolf). A gray wolf like Maugrim is larger than a red wolf or an Abyssinian wolf.

Band on the Run

In chapter 11 of *LWW*, C. S. Lewis mentions that Maugrim called a companion wolf to go on the hunt for the Beavers and the

Pevensies. Wolves live and hunt in packs of four to seven wolves within an established territory.

Like any wolf, Maugrim relied on his sense of smell to track his prey. (This is why he was the chief of the witch's secret police.) In fact, smell is a wolf's best sense (sight is the worst). A wolf's sense of smell is probably a hundred times greater than a human's.

Before heading out on the hunt, a wolf like Maugrim would've howled. That's part of a wolf's pre-hunt behavior. A whole pack of wolves will start howling before racing after prey. (They don't howl every time, however.)

They love the chase—especially the pursuit of weaker animals. They usually have more endurance than the animals they chase.

Lewis also mentions that Maugrim ran as fast as a horse can gallop. The average horse can run about 38 miles per hour (one of the fastest horses is the American quarter horse, which can run about 55 mph). Some wolves can run about 28–40 mph, but have to slow down after a while. A wolf usually travels at a pace of about 5–6 miles per hour.

Once a wolf pack finds the quarry, they quickly surround it. Sometimes they sit in a circle around the animal, waiting for it to panic and run away. If it runs, the wolves will chase it, hoping to tire it out.

A wolf may back off if an animal decides to stand and fight. That's what Bambi and Faline did in Disney's *Bambi*.

A Few Good Wolves

By now, you might be feeling a little sad about the way wolves are portrayed in stories (if you happen to like wolves). But the stories about wolves aren't all bad. Aside from movies like the *Shreks*, in which the big bad wolf is tamer and friendlier (well, he chases the pigs occasionally), some stories involve wolves with more positive images. The myth behind the founding of Rome is one such story.

In that story, a woman named Rhea Silvia, the daughter of a king, gave birth to twins: Romulus (who later founded Rome) and Remus. (The father of the twins was Mars, the Roman god of war.)

Now, Rhea's uncle Amulius took over the throne of Rhea's father. Amulius had the twins thrown into the River Tiber to stop them from gaining the throne someday. (Sound familiar? Check out chapter 8, where we talk about another person who tried to

All About Maugrim

WHERE WE FIRST MEET HIM: Chapter 9 (a note from him appears in chapter 6)

OTHER NAMES: In the British version of *LWW*, his name is Fenris Ulf.

QUALITIES/PHYSICAL CHARACTERISTICS: He's a large gray wolf, with a "great, red mouth" and "a growling voice." He's obedient to the White Witch and merciless to those he considers enemies. He can run as fast as a horse can gallop.

CLAIM TO FAME: Maugrim arrests Mr. Tumnus on behalf of the White Witch and is sent by her to kill the Pevensies and the Beavers. But Peter kills him instead, and gains the title "Sir Peter Wolf's-Bane."

LIKES/LOVES: Unknown

DISLIKES: Those disloyal to the White Witch

NARNIA TITLE(S): Captain/Chief of the Witch's secret police

harm a child in order to prevent him from becoming king.) But a female wolf found them and fed them until humans could adopt them.

That wolf wasn't the only foster mother to humans. Wolves also raised Mowgli, an orphaned boy in *The Jungle Book* by Rudyard Kipling.

If you saw the 1985 Disney movie *The Journey of Natty Gann*, you know all about how Natty Gann befriended a wolf as she searched for her father. This loyal wolf helped protect her during the journey.

And don't forget *White Fang*, a book by Jack London (1906) and a movie by Disney (1991). White Fang is three-quarters gray wolf and one-quarter husky. After being mistreated by a number of people, White Fang later meets Weedon Scott. Living with Scott teaches him about trust. After saving Scott's life, he's called "the Blessed Wolf" by the family, who come to love him.

A New Beginning

Let's switch gears and talk about spring. Spring was certainly a switch for the witch and animals like Maugrim who worked for her. Her plan was for it to be winter always (winter and never Christmas). Spring was a sign that her powers were diminishing and worst of all (in her evil mind) that Aslan was on the move. (The return of Father Christmas—see chapter 10 of this book— was another sign that Aslan was moving.) In chapter 11 of *LWW*, the witch was shocked to see the return of spring.

Remember what happened as the Beavers talked about Aslan in chapter 7 of *LWW*? Just the mention of Aslan's name caused at least three of the Pevensies (Peter, Susan, and Lucy) to feel hopeful. Although they hadn't yet met Aslan, they still felt a sense of wonder and peace at the mention of his name. (Edmund just felt sick.) They were just beginning to believe in him.

Spring has always been a time of new beginnings: buds on trees, new blossoms, young animals hatching, new butterflies, and so on. But this spring in Narnia also meant something bigger: that evil and winter *wouldn't* last forever. A new beginning *was* possible for Narnia. And the Pevensies' faith in Aslan, which was probably as tiny as the buds on trees, made a new beginning possible for them.

Satyrs

Perhaps you had some questions about the satyrs who celebrated Christmas (chapter 11 of *LWW*) or who fought against the White Witch (chapter 16). (For example, "What exactly *are* satyrs?")

C. S. Lewis didn't invent these creatures. They come from Greek myths. Satyrs are half man, half goat. They have the legs, horns, and ears of a goat, but the torso of a man.

Now wait. We know what you're thinking. Aren't *fauns* half man, half goat? Sure. But supposedly fauns are less mischievous than satyrs. Actually, some scholars believe that fauns and satyrs are the same creature.

Pan, the god of woods and hills in Greek mythology, looked somewhat like a satyr. But his son Silenus is probably the first official satyr. (Silenus is mentioned in chapter 2 of *LWW*.) Satyrs are followers of Silenus. Fauns come from Roman myths and supposedly are followers of the Roman god Faunus, who seems like Pan by any other name.

Many writers, such as Edmund Spenser (*The Faerie Queen*; see chapter 12) and Shakespeare, mention satyrs or Pan in their works.

Narnians You Wouldn't Want to Meet in a Dark Alley

- Maugrim

- The White Witch

- The Dwarf

- Any of the evil creatures mentioned in chapter 13 of this book

TA-DUH!

Much Ado About Moss

Edmund wondered whether moss would later grow on the statues the spiteful witch made out of the satyrs and animals. The answer is, yes (if they remained statues). As you probably know, moss (a *bryophyte,* which is a green plant without seeds) grows on the north sides of trees, rocks, and stone walls. Why the north side? The north side is the shaded side.

The moisture and acidic nature of rocks cause these tiny plants to form. Once they form, they spread by producing spores. If you look hard enough, you'll see the tiny leaves and stems of moss. (Okay, you probably need a microscope to see them.)

Think all mosses looks alike? Think again! There are many different types of mosses—at least 10,000 different kinds. Fringe moss is the kind that grows on stone walls and rocks. About thirty different kinds can be found in Great Britain.

By the way: the moss that grows on the north sides of trees is an alga.

CHAPTER TWELVE

A Knight's Tale

The Peck of Perils Peter Pevensie Picked

Princes in our world come in flavors like Charles, William, Harry (England); Hashim bin Hussein (Jordan); and Louis (Luxembourg). They drive cars, play polo, attend groundbreakings of hospitals and other buildings, do charity work, and hold press conferences. Occasionally, they've been asked to apologize for something bad they've done. But usually, they aren't asked to kill a wolf to "win their spurs" (see "Spur Winning" below) as Peter does in chapter 12 of *LWW*.

Ever been thrown into the deep end of a pool? You either swim or sink. That's how it was for Peter (not literally). He barely had time to react before his first battle with a wolf he at first thought was an Alsatian (a German shepherd). After being given a sword and a shield, and soon after he arrived at the Stone Table, he had to fight or die. Imagine how you would feel in that situation. (Imagine being given a sword—how cool is that?)

FROM ZERO TO HERO

To think that Peter was an ordinary kid, who probably never dreamed he would have to fight a wolf or become a prince all in one day. See, that's the beauty of a fairy tale. You wake up ordinary one day and a prince or princess the next. (Hey, it happened to Mia Thermopolis in the Princess Diaries series by Meg Cabot. Maybe it could happen to you. Have you taken the test in chapter 4 to see what kind of ruler you would be? If not, why not do it now?)

There are many fairy tales involving commoners who become royal by marrying royalty (Cinderella, Snow White, and Beauty/Belle of *Beauty and the Beast* marry princes; and countless named and unnamed young men marry princesses). In other stories, some people discover that some evil castle worker or family member snatched them away from their royal parents when they were babies. So, they were royal all along!

Not Peter. Aslan, the real "High King" of Narnia, made him "royal." Once royal, he would always be royal—an honor he shared with his brother and sisters.

In English society, the firstborn of a titled family (duke, viscount, earl) usually inherits the title. That person cannot share it with, say, the second born. The second born, while respectable, would only receive the title if something happened to the firstborn. So, as the firstborn offspring of Prince Charles, William, the Prince of Wales, will be king. His brother Harry will only be king if something happens to William.

But in Narnia, all four Pevensies are considered kings and queens. Peter is the High King or the king who ranks higher in authority than all the others. (Check out "All About Peter" at the end of this chapter.)

SPUR WINNING

Remember how Aslan said that Peter had to "win his spurs"? You might wonder what exactly that means. When knights used to wear armor centuries ago (and occasionally at medieval fairs in our day), they wore spurs. If you've seen a western, you've seen a cowboy wear spurs. The spurs of medieval times looked sort of like those. (Or we should say western spurs looked sort of like the spurs of medieval times, since those came first.) Spurs were the last piece of armor given to a young man who earned the right to be called a knight.

The phrase *win his spurs* comes from that tradition. It means "prove yourself worthy of knighthood by doing something brave." Back in the Middle Ages, during the time of knights and all, a young man was given a set of gold spurs (to go with his armor) when he was knighted. So, achieving knighthood earned him those spurs. A knight or prince had to win them by winning his first battle or accomplishing his first task as a knight. This was like a rite of passage—something every young knight had to go through.

During the knighting ceremony, after the armor was placed on the knight, he was then struck by the flat of the sword on his neck or shoulder. This action wasn't rude, it was a tradition. Aslan did this for Peter, after Peter defeated Maugrim. He also named him "Sir Peter Wolf's-Bane." Besides the fact that wolf's-bane is a poisonous plant, in this case it means something like "a foe of wolves."

St. George and C. S. Lewis

Peter's fight with Maugrim reminds us of another epic fight: that of the Red Cross Knight who fought a dragon. Maybe you've heard at least part of the story. He was called "the Red Cross Knight," because of the red cross on his shield. (Actually, he didn't know his own name.) Remember back in chapter 5b, when we told you about a knight's coat of arms? A cross was the symbol of a Crusader.

See, a princess (Una, who has a dwarf as her servant) went in search of a knight to kill a dragon terrorizing her land. (You don't see those every day.) The Fairy Queen sent the Red Cross Knight on this quest. While they travel back to her homeland, they encounter many adventures.

Back in the sixteenth century, an English poet named Edmund Spenser wrote an epic (a long narrative poem) called *The Faerie Queen*, which tells the story of the Red Cross Knight and others. This knight may have been patterned after St. George, a real person, who was killed in the fourth century because of his Christian beliefs. St. George, a former Roman soldier, is considered the patron saint of England, thanks to King Edward III. Not much is known about his life. Yet he had a reputation for being a warrior-saint, who quite possibly never set foot in England. (Another man, an Italian priest called Jacobus de Voragine, also wrote about St. George and the dragon in a collection of legends called the *Golden Legend*.)

The Faerie Queen is considered one of the greatest poems ever written. (Perhaps you have a different opinion.) With this poem, Spenser started a new trend in poetry with his nine-line stanza (called "the Spenserian stanza"; hey, you might hear about it in language arts someday).

C. S. Lewis was very familiar with and inspired by *The Faerie Queen*. Remember back in chapter 5a, when we told you that a man named Kirkpatrick tutored C. S. Lewis? Well, Lewis read *The Faerie Queen* during his time with Kirkpatrick.

After reading *Faerie Queen*, Lewis wrote a short story called "Bleheris," which was about a young knight named—you guessed it—Bleheris (don't ask us how he came up with that name) on a quest. His companions on the quest were a dwarf (just like Una's companion in *The Faerie Queen*) and a squirrel named Nut. (Does that remind you of a Beatrix Potter book? If not, turn back to chapter 5c.)

Lewis included in his story a character named Wan Jadis, a man who helps Bleheris on his quest. But many years later, Lewis gave part of his name to the White Witch.

NAIADS AND DRYADS

Lewis mentions naiads and dryads at Aslan's camp during Peter's battle with Maugrim. Naiads and dryads come from Greek myths. Naiads (also known as *nymphs*) are spirits living in the water, while dryads are spirits living in trees. They're usually on the side of good.

Naiads and dryads can take physical form. They're always beautiful young women. But don't confuse a naiad with a mermaid or a Nereid (a sea nymph).

Dryads die when their trees die (for example, if their trees are cut down). Yet they can live a long time.

PETER, YOU'RE NOT THE ONLY ONE

In a number of stories (real life and fiction) many young people were caught up in the wars of their times. C. S. Lewis was another young man caught in a war. But we'll get to his story in chapter 16. For now, think about:

- David, a shepherd who was probably just a teen when he volunteered to fight Goliath, the seemingly unbeatable Philistine who challenged the army of the Israelites (1 Samuel 17 in the Bible)

- Joan of Arc, who was ready to go to war at age twelve. She waited until she was about seventeen, though, before she went (She later became the patron saint of France)

- Johnny Tremain (in the book that bears his name by Esther Forbes), a teen who became involved in the American Revolution.

- Anakin Skywalker (before he turned evil) was just half Peter's age when he was forced to fight in the war for the planet Naboo in *Star Wars, Episode 1*

- Four of the five children E. Nesbit wrote about (Cyril, Anthea, Robert, and Jane), who found themselves involved in Julius Caesar's campaign to conquer Britain in *The Amulet*

The Name's the Same

Peter is a pretty common name in stories and in real life. Why, there's

- Peter the Great (a Russian czar, 1672–1725)

- Peter Jackson (director of the *Lord of the Rings* movies)

- Peter Pan

- Peter and the Wolf

- Peter Ilich Tchaikovsky (the famous composer of music like *Swan Lake*)

- Simon Peter (a follower of Jesus)

The Promised Land

Ever been shown something you might receive as a reward for a job well done? Perhaps you were promised a video game or a trip somewhere if you made all A's or completed some other hard task. This glimpse of a future reward was encouragement for you to work harder or to accomplish a goal. That's what Aslan did for Peter as the future High King of Narnia. In chapter 12 of *LWW,* Aslan shows Peter Cair Paravel: a beautiful, shining castle. This is the reward he will receive after winning the battle against the witch. This goal is achieved by the end of the book.

Cair Paravel reminds us of other places in stories C. S. Lewis would have read. The first place we think of is the Celestial City in *Pilgrim's Progress* by John Bunyan. A man named Pilgrim kept seeing glimpses of this beautiful city during his journey. Someday he would live there forever. So, throughout the story, he headed in that direction. These glimpses of the Celestial City encouraged him to continue on his journey.

Celestial City was the Promised Land, much like Canaan— the land God promised Moses that He would give to the people of Israel if they stayed faithful to him (Exodus 3).

Heaven is another shining place like Cair Paravel. It's actually the ultimate place—the one Cair Paravel and Celestial City are patterned after. John, a follower of Jesus, saw a vision of a shining city in heaven (Revelation 21), when he was an old man exiled on an island.

The Stones of the UK

Stonehenge

The Stone Table, a sacred meeting place, reminded us of some of the standing stones found throughout the United Kingdom (especially in Northern Ireland, C. S. Lewis's homeland). Many Celtic legends surround these national monuments.

You've probably heard about Stonehenge: a ring of standing stones on Salisbury Plain in the county of Wiltshire, in southern England. This sacred meeting place appears in stories throughout the centuries. Many tourists, including C. S. Lewis, have visited the site. In a book of his brother Warren's diaries, there's a photo of Lewis taken at Stonehenge in 1925.[1]

Many people thought the Druids, an ancient group of priests from Gaul (now France and Belgium), built it. Really, no one knows who built this monument, only half of which still stands today. Whoever built it probably started around 3000 B.C. and the building continued in phases.

The stones are bluestone from the Preselli Mountains in Wales, and sandstone, which comes from the Marlborough Downs, at least twenty miles away. Amazingly, just one of the

---

[1] *Brothers and Friends: The Diaries of Major Warren Hamilton Lewis,* ed. Clyde S. Kilby and Marjorie Lamp Mead (San Francisco: Harper & Row, 1980).

bluestones probably weighs about 5 tons, while one of the larger sandstones might weigh about 45 tons! Each had to be dragged into place.

Stonehenge isn't the only monument of mystery. Have you heard of the Dolmen of the Four Maols? Don't worry if you haven't. The Dolmen of the Four Maols is a tomb near Ballina in Ireland. It's made up of four large stones—three at the base and one on top. Perhaps it was built around 2000 B.C. Supposedly, it is the tomb of four brothers who plotted to kill a bishop, their foster father. Their story has now become a legend.

Or, have you heard about the wedge tomb of Gleninsheen in Ireland, which dates back to 2500 B.C.? It's called a *wedge tomb* because of its shape.

All About Peter

AGE: Twelve

BIRTH ORDER: The oldest of the Pevensies

NICKNAME(S): Edmund called him and the rest of his siblings "self-satisfied prigs." Other than that, he doesn't seem to have a nickname beyond the Narnia titles on page 151.

QUALITIES: Peter seems to be a natural leader (Edmund, however, would describe him as bossy). He can be harsh, when someone makes him angry. When he is wrong, he owns up to it without a fuss. He is not one to jump into danger lightly. Yet when danger comes, he runs to meet it, even though he is afraid.

During the Golden Age of Narnia, Peter becomes a tall, deep-chested man who is known to be a great warrior

CLAIM TO FAME: He kills the wolf, Maugrim, in his first battle and helps win the battle against the witch.

LIKES/LOVES: He likes doing whatever he pleases. He seems to like exploring old houses and woods. Like Edmund (see chapter 9 of this book), he would've liked pulling apart the armor in the Professor's house if he had the chance.

DISLIKES: Edmund's spitefulness, which led Edmund to tease Lucy

GIFT FROM FATHER CHRISTMAS: A shield and a sword

NARNIA TITLE(S): Sir Peter Wolf's-Bane; King Peter; the High King; King Peter the Magnificent; Son of Adam

CHAPTER THIRTEEN

The Good, the Bad, and the Ugly

Monster Mash

Monsters Inc., the movie by Pixar, is a movie about monsters. (We're not telling you anything you don't already know.) But all of them seem tame compared to the really nasty ones found in chapter 13 and 14 of *LWW*. These chapters provide almost a Who's Who among mythical monsters.

The chapter isn't just about monsters, however. It shows some fairy-tale creatures on the side of good. (And we mean those creatures found only in myths, like centaurs and ogres. We don't mean beavers, eagles, deer, or dogs—even the talking ones—of Aslan's army. We talk about eagles and other birds in chapter 6 and beavers in chapter 7.) But you don't have to guess which side each creature is on. C. S. Lewis was pretty clear about that.

That's why we've split this list of fairy-tale creatures into the good, the bad, and the ugly. We've tried to give you a little background about these creatures: what they are and which stories feature them.[1] FYI: A lot of them are found in Greek and Roman

[1] Here we go with more of these tiny notes. We found lots of information on mythical creatures, thanks to a book by Carol Rose called *Spirits, Fairies, Leprechauns, and Goblins: An Encyclopedia* (New York: W. W. Norton & Co., 1996). See Web sites like http://www.factmonster.com, http://www.calormen.com/Calormen/encyclopedia.htm; http://www.frsd.k12.nj.us/copperteach/fifthgrade/old_stuff/herman/myths/dictiona.htm; and http://www.angelfire.com/wv/bonktea/creatures.html. (You know the drill; check with your parents before you go online.)

myths. Since C. S. Lewis learned Greek (and by Greek, we mean Ελληνικά) and Latin and read stories in those languages as part of his education, he would have known many of these stories.

We added an extra category for creatures that were not only bad but ugly as well, because we wanted to use the title of an old Clint Eastwood movie—*The Good, the Bad, and the Ugly*—as our chapter title. (Yeah, okay. You're not familiar with that one. But maybe your mom or dad is.) For some creatures, deciding which category they fit—the bad or the ugly—was difficult. Maybe after reading this list, you'll come up with your own categories.

THE GOOD

There's no question about it: some of the creatures most loyal to Aslan were centaurs and unicorns. Okay, you probably know something about them already. They're also pretty common in Greek myths and other stories. But we're still going to tell you a little bit about them.

CENTAURS A centaur is half man, half horse (a man's torso with a horse's limbs). We're sure you already know that, especially with a description like the one in chapter 12 of *LWW* (C. S. Lewis describes the centaurs as "stern but beautiful giants"—the human part—while the horse part is like "huge English farm horses"). You may even know that some centaurs have wings. But did you know that some are part man, part bull (*bucentaurs*) or that others are part donkey, part man (*onocentaurs*)? (Wonder what they eat?)

You can find centaurs (the kind that are half man, half horse) in many Greek myths, even though a group called the Kassites[2]

---

[2] Another source for mythical creatures is *Mythical and Fabulous Creatures: A Sourcebook and Research Guide*, Malcolm South, ed. (New York: Peter Bedrick Books, 1988).

probably made them up between 1750 and 1150 B.C. Somehow, centaurs wound up painted on a lot of vases in different cultures.

In the stories above, many of the centaurs were wild and mean. But two weren't. One of them, Cheiron (or Chiron, depending on what version of the *Iliad* you have), is mentioned in the *Iliad,* the epic poem by Homer. (The movie *Troy* was based on the *Iliad*.) Cheiron especially was kind, gentle, and intelligent. The centaurs in *LWW* seem patterned after him.

Speaking of the poet Homer, he's considered the first poet to use the word *centaur*. But he didn't exactly describe them as half man, half horse. Another Greek poet, a man named Pindar, is the first to describe them this way. He also wrote that the first centaurs (with the exception of Cheiron) were the offspring of a man named Ixion, who married a cloud he mistook for the goddess Hera (the wife of the ruling Greek god Zeus). (We don't know how he could have made that mistake.)

(Don't forget that centaurs and satyrs are not the same. We used to get those two mixed up. We talked about satyrs in chapter 11.)

UNICORNS What do you think of when you think of the unicorn?[3] A white horse with a horn on its head? Unicorns have been around in stories for thousands of years, especially in Greek myths. But Greek myths aren't the only stories about unicorns; many cultures have them. In the Greek stories, a unicorn is half horse, half goat. In other stories, unicorns look like antelopes. But in *LWW,* unicorns look like horses.

Unicorns are generally thought of as pure, gentle, magical creatures. They may have been patterned after animals with horns (rhinoceros, narwhal, antelope).

---

[3] Gail Gibbons wrote a fun book on unicorns. It is *Behold . . . the Unicorn* (New York: HarperCollins, 2002).

A Greek doctor and historian named Ctesias, who lived around 400 B.C., is possibly the first person to mention a horse with one horn. Many Chinese folklore writers also mentioned unicorns. But these creatures were made up of parts of other animals (the head of a deer or lion, the body of a deer or horse).

Two Christian writers, St. Ambrose and St. Basil, who lived in the fourth century declared that the unicorn, because of its purity, was a symbol for Christ. (Some people believe that the unicorn is mentioned in the Bible. But we couldn't find any mention of it.)

During medieval times, a group of unknown artists wove a series of seven tapestries called *The Hunt of the Unicorn*. The tapestries tell the story of a unicorn hunt. But the story has a double meaning: one that points to Jesus' death and resurrection.

THE BAD

Remember how C. S. Lewis mentioned that some of the creatures in the White Witch's army were so awful, grown-ups might not let you read the book? We can see why. These are the kinds of creatures that heroes and heroines go to war against. They're enough to give anyone nightmares. But giving you nightmares was not his mission.

By mentioning these creatures, Lewis showed the level of danger the Pevensies, Aslan, and the other good and loyal Narnians were in. The witch didn't want to talk things over. She wanted to destroy all who refused to worship her.

Remember how Elastigirl (Helen Parr) in *The Incredibles* warned her kids about Buddy's men? She told them that the men would not show restraint just because they were kids; they would try their best to kill them. Chapters 13 and 14 show that level of danger.

Lewis could write about these creatures because he believed that good was stronger than evil. As a Christian, he believed that his God, like Aslan, could triumph over any enemy.

BOGGLES Maybe you've read the Harry Potter series and thought that the boggles and boggarts are the same (the Harry Potter series mentions *boggarts; LWW* has *boggles*). Boggles and boggarts are spirits in the folklore of northern England. They seem the same, but have slight differences. Both boggles and boggarts can change their shape for an instant. They might appear as a person or an animal. They supposedly like to frighten travelers. Boggarts, however, seem to like to hang around particular homes and frighten the inhabitants. Neither a boggle nor a boggart is a particularly welcome guest.

CRUELS Cruels are evil spirits, with small, hairy bodies and long teeth. (Cruel is a good name for them.) Not much is known about them. Apparently, they come from English folklore. In Shakespeare's play *King Lear,* one character (Gloucester) possibly refers to them in the line "All cruels else subscribe" (Act III, scene VII). (We're not 100 percent sure of that, however.)

EFREETS Efreets, spirits seen in some Arabic myths, also are known as Afrits or Djinns—the bad ones. (Remember what we said about them in chapter 8? Feel free to go back.) They're huge and very powerful, shape-changing creatures who don't seem to like humans. In other words, they're very nasty.

GIANTS You probably know a number of fairy tales with giants. "Jack and the Beanstalk" is probably the most popular. (It's so popular, several people—including Andrew Lang—have adapted it.) "Jack the Giant Killer," also adapted by Andrew Lang for *The Blue Fairy Book* is well known (C. S. Lewis wrote about "Jack the Giant Killer" in an essay called "On Stories"). In the Harry Potter series, Hagrid comes from the race of giants.

Stories about giants come from many different sources: European folklore, Norse myths, and Greek myths. Think of the

Cyclops—the one-eyed man-eating giant in the *Odyssey*. (The *Encyclopaedia Britannica* lists him as a type of ogre. However, ogres and giants are related.)

So, we don't have to really tell you that giants are pretty tall—beyond the height of a basketball player. Giants can be good (like Hagrid) or bad. In some of the fairy tales by the Grimm brothers like "The Young Giant" and "The Giant and the Tailor," giants are pretty decent. (See, that's the great thing about having a book like *Grimms' Complete Fairy Tales*. You get to bring up stories people haven't heard and they think you're cool.) And in *LWW*, there is a good giant (Rumblebuffin). But in many stories, they're bad and not very intelligent. The White Witch in *LWW* recruited only evil ones for her army and turned the good ones into stone.

Some giants (like the one in "Jack and the Beanstalk" or the Cyclops) have a bad habit of eating people.

Stories of giants can also be found in an unexpected source: the Bible. These giants are mentioned at least four times. David battled a giant over nine feet tall: Goliath (1 Samuel 17; he had a brother). Later, David and his men battled other giants, some of whom were related to Goliath (2 Samuel 21:15–22).

Ages before that, before the Flood even, men like giants roamed the earth (Genesis 6:4). Later, when the Israelites tried to enter Canaan (the Promised Land we told you about in chapter 12), they claimed to see giants (Numbers 13:28).

HORRORS These creatures seek to terrify their victims with their horrible, blood-curdling shrieks. They're supposedly difficult to see at night, because their color matches the night sky.

INCUBUSES An incubus is an evil spirit that sometimes takes the shape of a handsome man to fool unsuspecting women. Stories of these prowling spirits have been told since medieval times.

ORKNIES These small, sharp-nosed, mischievous creatures are believed to inhabit basements in some folklore. (Don't worry. There are no orknies in your basement.)

PEOPLE OF THE TOADSTOOLS These small creatures live in enchanted mushrooms. But they don't seem to be leprechauns or fairies. They're pretty evil, though.

SPECTERS These are ghosts—and very nasty ones at that. They're much more powerful than wraiths (see further along).

Some writers use words like *specter, wraith,* or *ghost* interchangeably.

SPRITES Although less powerful creatures like elves, pixies, and fairies are sometimes called sprites because of their mischievous behavior, *these* sprites are small, supernatural creatures that are never good and friendly. They're enemies of the tree spirits (the dryads).

WEREWOLVES You probably have heard that a werewolf is a human who has been transformed into a wolf after being bitten by another werewolf. He or she assumes the shape of a wolf when the full moon rises. But this sort of transformation (from man to wolf) doesn't always occur in some werewolf stories.

Werewolf stories in some form or other are as old as Greek myths (in other words, thousands of years old). You can also find some wolf stories in Norse myths (as we mentioned in chapter 11).

Many cultures, especially those in Western Europe, have werewolf stories. But these are quite different from the ones you've probably read. Some of these involve a man simply putting on a wolf skin in order to disguise himself. In others, being transformed into a wolf for a time is a punishment given out by an angry god.

In the first century, a Roman writer wrote a story about a soldier who was transformed from a human to a wolf. This story is closer to the werewolf stories of today.

Over the centuries, the legend of the werewolf grew, along with suggested different ways of eliminating a werewolf (silver bullet, burning at the stake). Silver objects can't kill some werewolves, however. Perhaps the werewolves in *LWW* are like that.

Wondering which is the first English werewolf story? "Hugues, the Wer-Wolf," a magazine story by Sutherland Menzies written in 1838. But a story called "The White Wolf of the Hartz Mountains," by a British naval commander, Captain Frederick Marryat, written in 1839, is better known. That story takes place in Transylvania—the location for many monster stories.

WRAITHS Wraiths are smokelike ghosts that can sometimes be seen in fog. In some stories, wraiths are believed to suck the breath out of a victim. They're very powerful and very evil. (In *Lord of the Rings*, nine creatures known as the "Ringwraiths" chased Frodo and his friends.)

THE UGLY

In chapter 13 of *LWW*, the witch declares that the sight of some of her army would turn men to stone (like the sight of Medusa). We don't doubt her words when we see the list that follows.

ETTINS Ettins are related to the giants and are known to fight with clubs. Some have two or three heads. None are pleasant to be around.

A story called "The Red Ettin," in Andrew Lang's *Blue Fairy Book*, features—you guessed it—an ettin.

GHOULS These creatures are evil spirits in stories that feed on dead bodies and rob graves. Pretty nasty, huh? In some Hindu folktales, they're a kind of Jinn.

HAGS This is an evil being, usually a witch, who takes the form of an exceptionally hideous old woman. Hags are found in many Celtic myths and other stories around the world. (Baba Yaga, the witch in many Russian folk tales, is a hag.)

In *Macbeth,* a play written by William Shakespeare in 1605–06, the main character, Macbeth (who schemes to kill the King of Scotland and take over the throne) calls the three witches "hags." (FYI: If you saw *Harry Potter and the Prisoner of Azkaban,* you heard a song by a children's choir. That song is based on the words of the witches in *Macbeth.*)

MINOTAURS Where do we begin with this one? We have to go back to a Greek myth: the story of a young man named Theseus. In that story, we find the original Minotaur, a creature part man, part bull. (These are not to be confused with the half man, half bull in chapter 12, of *LWW* who was still loyal to Aslan. That creature had a man's head and a bull's body.) Believe it or not, this creature was the son of a king—Minos of Crete. (That's a long story.)

You see, the Minotaur had a taste for humans. (Ugh.) So, a man named Daedalus made a labyrinth—maze—to keep the Minotaur in. Every nine years Minos took fourteen human sacrifices from Athens to feed to the Minotaur. (Some dads spoil their kids.)

Theseus, a wandering hero who just happened to kill monsters, was the son of the King of Athens. He offered to take the place of one of the people who was about to be sent to the Minotaur. To make a long story short, Theseus killed the Minotaur with the help of Ariadne, the daughter of Minos.

So, the minotaurs of Narnia are creatures with bull heads and the bodies of men. They pretty much act like the original one in the Greek myth.

OGRES If you saw the *Shrek* movies or *Ella Enchanted,* you saw ogres. These creatures turn up regularly in fairy tales, especially those from Eastern Europe. Although these aren't the lovable, Shrek variety, villagers would be tempted to chase them away with pitchforks all the same.

No one really knows who came up with ogres first. Was it the French writer Charles Perrault, who mentions an ogre in his fairy-tale collection (in the story "Puss in Boots")? Was the word first used when the *Arabian Nights* was translated into English in 1713? Regardless of who first coined the term, all agree that most ogres are smelly, human-flesh-eating creatures related to the giants (but not as tall). (Okay, Shrek didn't eat people. But the ogres in *Ella Enchanted* did.) They're not considered very bright. (You don't want man-eating creatures to be smart!)

Howard Pyle, in his fairy-tale collection *The Wonder Clock,* includes a story called "The Three Little Pigs and the Ogre." Instead of hunting for humans, the ogre turns his attention to—that's right—three little pigs.

WOOSES You might think *moose* when you see the word *woose.* A woose is a large, gray, hairless creature that looks like a stone. Only it isn't. If a person sat on one by accident, it would probably be the last thing he or she did in life.

There! That's quite a list to avoid reading at night just before you go to bed!

What's Deep Magic?

Wondering about the deep or the deeper magic Aslan mentions in chapter 13 of *LWW*? Besides being magic that isn't shallow (get it?), deep magic reminds us of the law described in the Bible. Breaking the law of the land (which Edmund did when he betrayed his family) was punishable by death in Narnia. But Aslan died instead of Edmund.

According to ancient Jewish law—laws established by the God of Israel—the punishment for any wrongdoing was death. But an animal (a lamb or bird) could be given instead, so that the person who did the wrong would not have to die. This was called a *sacrifice*. But these animals had to be perfect—no blemishes of any kind.

The whole thing started when Adam and Eve disobeyed God by eating from the tree he told them not to eat from. Their story is told in the third chapter of Genesis, the first book of the Bible (God's command to avoid eating from this tree is found in Genesis 2:16–17). Because of what they did wrong, they were separated from God. Everyone born after them had the same problem.

But Jesus' death during the first century ended the need for animal sacrifices. His death was the one perfect sacrifice that would count for all of the wrong things ever done. That's why he's called the "lamb of God" (see John 1:29).

(FYI: At the end of *Voyage of the Dawn Treader*, Aslan takes the form of a lamb. Maybe you noticed that.)

Aslan knew the law and honored it. After all, he was the son of the Emperor-Beyond-the-Sea, who made the laws. He knew that his willingness to die for Edmund would break the power of death and send him back to life.

The White Witch with her demand for Edmund's life is like Lucifer, a former angel whom the Bible says has access to heaven still. There he makes accusations against people (see Job 2:1).

C. S. Lewis wasn't trying to teach Sunday School with this story. His goal was to tell a great story. But he wanted that story to show his beliefs.

FIRE-STONES

The "fire-stones on the Secret Hill" that the witch mentions in chapter 13 are like the stone tablets upon which were written the Ten Commandments. Moses was given those tablets on Mount Sinai (Exodus 31:18). God carved the words in stone.

The Saddest Chapter Ever

It's Over Now?

Has someone ever said to you, "It's always darkest before the dawn"? If so, perhaps you shook your head and either wondered what that person was talking about (if you didn't know) or just went on about your business.

But that sentence is what we call an *idiom,* a phrase or statement that has a certain meaning to a group of people. Every culture has some. That's why if we said, "Whassup?" to you, you wouldn't look up. You'd know we meant "Hi" or "How are you?"

It's always darkest before the dawn means "Things always seem worse before they get better."

In chapter 14 of *LWW,* things couldn't possibly get worse. This is the point of the story where the villain seems to have the upper hand. It's the darkest moment for a hero or heroine. This also is the point of the story known as the *climax.* It's the "point of the greatest intensity . . . the turning point in a plot or dramatic action," according to the *American Heritage College Dictionary.* The action starts to move quickly from that point on.

What happens in chapter 14 goes beyond the standard action for a hero. Aslan, the only hope the Narnians have to defeat the Witch, is captured and killed by the witch. He doesn't just fall unconscious or become wounded as do so many heroes in books and movies. He dies. That's why this chapter is the saddest chapter in the book.

If Saruman the wizard from *Lord of the Rings* had been on the scene, he would have said, "There will be no dawn for men," just as he said in the movie version of *The Two Towers*.

That's certainly how the White Witch seems to act. As far as she was concerned, it is all over now. She has won. As far as Susan and Lucy, who followed Aslan, are concerned, it is all over. They witnessed the capture and torture of Aslan. What good could possibly come out of that?

Have you ever lost someone you cared about? Then you know just how they felt. C. S. Lewis certainly did. After all, his mom died just before he turned ten. Some of his friends died during World War I (see chapter 16). So, he was no stranger to grief. (His wife also died after four years of marriage. But he wrote *LWW* before his marriage.)

In this chapter, Lewis not only tells what happened to Aslan, he also shows someone else's story: that of Jesus. The suffering Aslan experienced just before his death is similar to (but not exactly like) that of Jesus described in the Bible around the time of the Jewish holiday called Passover.

Here's how the two stories are similar:

ASLAN	JESUS
• Felt sad, knowing what he had to go through (torture and death)	• Felt sad, knowing what he had to go through (torture and death) (Matthew 26:38)
• Wanted someone to be with him during this hard time	• Wanted someone to be with him during this hard time (Matthew 26:36–38)
• Was beaten and humiliated by his enemies, before being killed	• Was beaten and humiliated by his enemies, before being killed (Matthew 27)

Aslan and Jesus also are similar in the way they thought of others. Aslan still took time to talk over battle strategy with Peter, even though he was about to die. He was a king who cared about his creatures.

In the same way, while dying on the Cross, Jesus still made sure his mother had a home to go to (John 19:26–27).

Too Late?

The White Witch believed that Aslan's efforts to save Edmund were doomed to failure. That's why she felt free to gloat before killing Aslan.

Sometimes the efforts of a helpful hero seem to be too little, too late. Like Boromir in *The Fellowship of the Ring* (the first book/movie of *Lord of the Rings*), who tried and failed to save the hobbits from the orcs. Or like Gandalf in the same book (and movie) who defeated the balrog (you'll have to read that book to find out more about *that*), but couldn't save himself.

It was the same with Jesus. Some of the people in the crowd at his Crucifixion jeered at him, saying, "He saved others, but can't save himself" (Mark 15:31–32). As far as they were concerned, Jesus was just another failure.

We groan when we see Beauty (Belle in the Disney version) racing back to the castle of the Beast, only to see him lying there, seemingly dead. Were her efforts to get back doomed to failure?

We cry along with Aragorn, Pippin, and all the others when we see Frodo's mithril shirt in the hands of the enemy in *Return of the King* (Book 3 of Tolkien's trilogy). It looks like all hope is lost.

Overconfident Villains

Sometimes villains act almost overconfident in their belief that no one can stand in their way—certainly not the hero or heroine. But that overconfidence is sometimes fear that something will go terribly wrong with their evil plans. Perhaps that's why the witch had a great crowd of extremely evil beings near her when Aslan surrendered himself in chapter 14 (there's safety in numbers).

She's not the only overconfident villain.

- In *Two Towers* (the movie version of Book 2 of Tolkien's series), Saruman sent 10,000 orcs to battle 300 soldiers. That's like trying to kill a mosquito with a cannon.

- The evil queen in "Snow White" (Grimm version), after killing Snow White with a poisoned apple (after a number of attempts before that caused us to question Snow White's sanity, since she kept letting her in), went skipping happily off to her magic mirror, glad that she was finally the fairest in the land.

- Putting Briar Rose to sleep and ruining her life wasn't enough for Maleficent, the evil fairy in *Sleeping Beauty* (the Disney version). She had to turn into a dragon and fight the prince, too. She couldn't leave well enough alone.

A Sad Battle in Britain's History

As we mentioned earlier, Aslan told Peter about his strategy for the upcoming battle with the witch and her army. He didn't want them to lose this battle. Yet Peter and his siblings didn't have much hope of victory without Aslan.

If you've ever played chess, you know the importance of having a good battle strategy. If you don't, you can't defeat your opponent. And when you have an opponent like the White Witch, you need all the strategy you can get.

Wars are won or lost based on strategy. Every good general or commanding officer has to give thought to a good battle strategy (this is what Aslan tells Peter in chapter 14). Maybe you've played one of those war video games (like the *Lord of the Rings* games) that simulate a real battle. (There's even one based on the Battle of Britain, the battle we talked about in chapter 1.)

One of the most important battles in Britain's history is the Battle of Hastings—one that they lost on October 14, 1066. The Normans (Danes who settled in France) invaded England and changed British life forever, all because their commander had a better strategy.

William the Conqueror, who at one point was the Duke of Normandy, claimed that he was the successor to the throne of England. (Edward the Confessor, the previous king, had died.) Harold Godwinson, the earl of Wessex and the brother-in-law of Edward also claimed that the throne belonged to him. When a council of advisers named Harold the new king, William decided to fight for the throne. (With a name like William the Conqueror, you don't expect him to simply milk cows or churn butter or something.) He came up with a plan for battle during the winter of 1066, before gathering his troops to invade the land. The first place they landed across the English Channel was called Pevensey. (Does that name sound familiar? Think Pevensie.)

Another guy, Harald Hardrada of Norway, also thought the throne belonged to him. So, he gathered some troops to fight for the throne.

Harold, the commander of the English troops, was not as prepared as William. Yet his troops defeated Harald Hardrada's army (at Stamford Bridge), which might have caused him to feel over-confident. Even though his troops fought hard against William's troops, they couldn't keep up the pace. Finally, William's troops broke through their line and killed Harold. After his death, his troops basically gave up. England was conquered.

William's months and months of preparation paid off.

And in This Corner . . .

Think the White Witch is evil? Yeah she was (see "All About the White Witch" on page 170). As we said in chapter 13, she's like Lucifer, the former angel in the Bible who rebelled against God.

The White Witch comes from a long tradition of evil villains. A villain who seems almost impossible to beat adds suspense to a story. But how does she rate against other evil villains in fiction? Villains like

- Dracula from the book of the same name by Bram Stoker (an evil, undead, bloodthirsty creature determined to "live" forever)

- The Wicked Witch of the West from *The Wonderful Wizard of Oz* (her name says it all)

- Sauron (evil Lucifer-like character in *The Lord of the Rings;* the true "lord of the ring")

- Voldemort (evil warlock in the Harry Poter series)

Let's consult our handy evil-ometer and see what results we find.

EVIL-OMETER

10.2	10	9	8	7	6	5	4	3	2	1

▲ JADIS (THE WHITE WITCH)

▲ SAURON

　　DRACULA ▲

　　　　▲ WICKED WITCH OF THE WEST

　　▲ VOLDEMORT

Sauron seems to just edge out Jadis and Voldemort (in our opinions) as the most evil villain, even though he shared some of the same goals as Voldemort and Jadis (power, world domination, exploiting the weak). But don't feel sorry for Jadis or Voldemort. After all, they are *still* evil. Dracula comes in next, with the Wicked Witch of the West after that. Dracula at least was human at one point and expressed feelings of loneliness. And the Wicked Witch of the West is described as a decent decorator. But they're still evil.

How would you rank them?

All About the White Witch

REAL NAME: Jadis (you can find this in *The Magician's Nephew*)

WHERE WE FIRST MEET HER: In *The Magician's Nephew*

QUALITIES/PHYSICAL CHARACTERISTICS: Tall; has a complexion like snow or chalk and a red mouth; evil. She lacks even one "drop of real human blood," according to the Beavers. She is a descendant of Lilith, "the first wife of Adam" (see chapter 8 in this book for more on this myth)

CLAIM TO FAME: Turns Narnia into a permanent winter wonderland (but never Christmas); kills Aslan

GOALS: (1) To rule Narnia forever; (2) to get rid of the Pevensies in order to make goal 1 happen; (3) to get rid of Aslan to make goal 1 happen

LIKES/LOVES: Being evil

DISLIKES: Aslan and his followers

NARNIA TITLE(S): The White Witch; Queen of Narnia and Empress of the Lone Islands (she calls herself this)

Chillin' Like a Villain Quiz

These classic villains (old and new; from books and movies) would probably side with the witch if they were in this book. Can you guess who they are? We warn you, these are challenging. The words in italics are clues, but not always about the villain's name. Sometimes the words are clues to the book or movie that he or she is from. For example, if we were to say, "*A lad who made an awful din* told us about this villain who wouldn't go *far*," who would you guess? Jafar from *Aladdin!* (Alad + din = Aladdin. And *far* is an easy clue that points to Jafar. But the clues below won't be this easy—we hope!)

If you don't know one of the stories listed below, we hope this quiz encourages you to read it.

1. When it comes to this villain, *never never* ask him to give you a *hand*. (But you might take him *fishing*.)

2. She's *crueler* than a junkyard *dog*.

3. He couldn't stand the *robbin'*. He needed *a rest* from it, because his stomach was in *knots*.

4. Ar, *Jim*, this villain *isn't golden*. *I'll* bet he's the kind of friend who'd betray ya, instead of *treasuring* you.

5. You might ask your local *bard* about the weakness of this villain. This *treasure* stealing villain was a *drag on* a small person, who had a *habit* of disappearing.

6. We'd be *lyin'* if we said this villain didn't leave a *mark* on us.

7. You couldn't *dodge* this *pickpocket*-training *Victorian* villain.

8. The *lead* villain caused teens to really *dig* this book. And that's the *whole* truth. (Don't *miss*-take this villain.)

9. When it comes to *family* villains, we *three* can *count* on him.

10. He was *dying* to work against the *hero* who wasn't a *zero*.

11. In this *enchanting* movie, this villain would be a *Slytherin* if he were in Harry Potter.

12. The *force* was not with this man behind the *mask*.

ANSWERS

1. Captain Hook in *Peter Pan* by J. M. Barrie

2. Cruella De Vil in *101 Dalmatians* (book by Dodie Smith; Disney movie)

3. The Sheriff of Nottingham in *Robin Hood* by various adapters, including Roger Lancelyn Green and Howard Pyle

4. Long John Silver in *Treasure Island* by Robert Louis Stevenson

5. Smaug in *The Hobbit* by J. R. R. Tolkein (Bard is a character is that book; the small person is the hobbit Bilbo.)

6. Scar in *The Lion King* (Disney)

7. Fagin in *Oliver Twist* by Charles Dickens

8. The Warden in *Holes* by Louis Sachar

9. Count Olaf of Lemony Snicket's Series of Unfortunate Events books

10. Hades in *Hercules* (Disney version)

11. Heston the snake the *Ella Enchanted*

12. Darth Vader in the *Star Wars* movies

CHAPTER FIFTEEN

The "Mane" Event

Eucatastrophe and You

You know what a disaster feels like, right? Miserable. But have you ever experienced a time when a disaster was suddenly overturned? How did you feel then? Joyful—relieved?

J. R. R. Tolkien made up a word for that: *eucatastrophe*.[1] Sounds a bit like *supercalifragilisticexpialidocious* (from *Mary Poppins*), doesn't it? (Well, maybe not quite.) *Eucatastrophe* is a big, impressive word that describes a sudden action or event in a story that changes defeat into victory. This event is so wonderful, it causes a character to cry out of joy. A happy ending can now take place.

For example, let's say you've been totally humiliated by a fellow student—someone who treats you like a flea for most of the school year. Week after week you're embarrassed in front of everyone. *Catastrophe!* But all of a sudden the principal catches this person in action and announces to the whole school that your enemy will be transferred to a school in a

---

[1] Here we are, troubling your reading with another footnote. How naughty of us. But we wanted to tell you that Tolkien mentions this word in a letter he wrote and in an essay called "On Fairy-Stories," which is part of a book called *Essays Presented to Charles Williams*, edited by C. S. Lewis (Grand Rapids, MI: William B. Eerdmans, 1966; first published 1947 by Oxford University Press).

country far, far away! (And not like the kingdom of Far, Far Away in *Shrek 2!*) What's more, your calmness and perseverance in the face of adversity make you a hero to many at school. Suddenly you're the most popular person at school! (If you're an adult reading this, substitute *work* for *school*.) *Eucatastrophe!*

According to Tolkien (and C. S. Lewis agrees), the best fairy tales show this kind of reversal. In that moment of joy when a character finally realizes that everything will turn out right, you (the reader) can sense a greater truth: that good *does* triumph over evil. That's why we're relieved when, after all of Cinderella's suffering at the hands of her nasty stepmother and stepsisters, the prince shows up at her door with her glass slipper in his hand. That's why we go, "Woo hoo!" when the Beast revives after Beauty returns to his castle. That's why we say, "Yes!" when the ring and Sauron are destroyed in *Lord of the Rings*.

A Big Event

Guess what event turns everything around in *LWW*? That's right. Aslan's return to life in chapter 15 (the "deeper magic" of the book) is the event that turns the White Witch's triumph (chapter 14) into the beginning of her total defeat. This is the "mane" event of the book.

Since Lewis already showed how Aslan's death was similar in some ways to Jesus' death, it's only fitting that Aslan's return to life should have some similarities to Jesus' resurrection, too. That story is told in Matthew 28, Mark 16, Luke 24, and John 20.

Check this out:

ASLAN	JESUS
• Susan and Lucy went to the Stone Table to wash Aslan's wounds after his death.	• Two Marys went to the tomb to wash and anoint his body for burial (Matthew 28:1–8).
• They discovered Aslan's body was missing.	• They discovered an empty tomb.
• Aslan suddenly appeared, alive once more.	• An angel told them that Jesus was alive.

Like the women who went to Jesus' tomb, Susan (check out "All About Susan" at the end of the chapter) and Lucy once again bravely went where no one else dared to go. Imagine how surprised, shocked, and confused they felt when they discovered the Stone Table empty, just as the women discovered the empty tomb. But Susan and Lucy also discovered the event that made everything better: Aslan was alive!

There are other ways that Aslan's return to life is similar to Jesus'. The broken Stone Table is like the curtain in the Temple in the Jerusalem of Jesus' day. This curtain tore in two the moment Jesus died (Matthew 27:51). Wondering why this curtain tore? Well, the curtain was there in the first place to show the separation between people and God. Because Jesus, an innocent man, died for the wrongs all people committed (Romans 5:7–10), there was no longer a separation between people and God. This is what Lewis believed. This is "the deeper magic" of Narnia (see "What's Deep Magic?" in chapter 13).

Aslan did what Boromir in *Fellowship of the Ring* (we mentioned him in chapter 14) couldn't do: save someone. Because Aslan died for Edmund, the Stone Table broke in half. The Stone Table was like Golgotha, the place where Jesus was put to death. An earthquake happened just as Jesus died, tearing the land in two (Matthew 27:51).

For C. S. Lewis, the hope created in Lucy and Susan by Aslan's return to life is the hope he had about his own life. Even though his life was hard at times, he still had hope that the God he believed in would triumph at the end.

Aslan's return to life didn't mean that all battles were over. After all, the White Witch was still present with her army of evil. Peter and Edmund would still have to fight this army (see chapter 16). But ultimately, the victory was theirs even before the battle began. Why? Because Aslan was alive. If he could come back from the dead, he could certainly defeat the White Witch and her crew. (By the way, we can't resist bringing up another resurrection: that of Gandalf in *Two Towers*. His return brought hope to Aragorn and others.)

He's Alive!

Incidentally, the fact that Susan and Lucy wondered whether or not Aslan was a ghost reminded us of the reaction of Jesus' followers when they saw him alive again. The Bible describes their reactions. Those who thought he was a ghost (Luke 24:37) were terrified! (Wouldn't you be?) But, like Aslan, he touched them and ate with them to assure them that he wasn't a ghost (Luke 24:38–43).

One guy, Thomas, refused to believe that Jesus was alive until he could touch Jesus' wounds. So, one day, Jesus appeared and told Thomas to touch his wounds (see John— the fourth book of the New Testament—chapter 20, starting at verse 24).

Run, Cat, Run!

In chapter 15 of *LWW,* after Aslan returns to life, he invites Susan and Lucy to take a ride on his back. We couldn't help thinking of the Oz stories by L. Frank Baum. In those stories Dorothy and others often rode on the back of the Cowardly Lion.

Could you ride a lion? Possibly. An adult lion (male) can weigh about 300 to 500 pounds. So, he could definitely hold your weight and easily run with you. But the question is, would he *let* you ride him?

As to how smooth the ride might be, that's hard to say. We can say that a lion is a *digitigrade.* That means he or she walks on his toes. His/her heel doesn't touch the ground when it walks.

Since C. S. Lewis compared the riding styles of a horse and a lion, we decided to look into that more. We discovered that a horse's body frame is more stable than a lion's. A horse has less muscle and more tendons in its limbs than a lion does. It also has more vertebrae, which makes for a more rigid back. When it runs, its hooves solidly hit the ground. When it falls asleep standing up, its back doesn't sink under its own weight.

A lion has more flexibility, because it is more muscular. It can't fall asleep while standing, because it would collapse. Yet a lion can easily curl up on the ground or on a large rock, while a horse has difficulty.[2]

If you read chapter 15 of *LWW,* you remember how Aslan ran and ran. (He's no ordinary lion!) When a lion runs, its spine expands and contracts. It can run about 29–35 miles per hour and leap over 30 feet. While a lion can be a powerful sprinter,

[2] A great Web site deals with this very subject: http://natureinstitute.org/txt/ch/horselion.htm. (Are you checking with your parents? Good.)

normally it doesn't like to run long distances. It will run about 100 or so yards, then stop. That's why lions hunt in groups.

Lewis mentions that Aslan runs faster than the fastest race-horse. As we told you in chapter 11, one of the fastest horses is the quarter horse, which runs at 55 mph. So, you can imagine that he runs pretty fast. Maybe "Whirlwind" should be his nickname!

TA-DUH!

More Lion Facts

Okay, you noticed Aslan roaring in chapter 15. But did you know that lions are one of four cats that roar? The other three are jaguars, leopards, and tigers. They roar because of a two-piece bone in their throats called a *hyoid* bone. A lion's roar can supposedly be heard five miles away.

Also, did you know that lions are the only cats with tassels on their tails? Cool, huh?

What We Need Is . . . a Hero(ine) Quiz

In many stories, the hero or heroine sacrifices his/her time and sometimes his/her life to save or help someone else. That's all part of being a hero(ine). Think about the firefighters or police officers you see on the news or racing by on the street. They risk their lives every day.

Many heroes and heroines (even the ordinary ones) have virtues or special abilities that enable them to complete their quests. For example, sheer love compelled Aslan to sacrifice his life for Edmund.

Believe it or not, the pairs of heroes and heroines below have a virtue or special ability in common. What quality do you think each pair has? To help you out, here are some lists of qualities.

- Love, joy, peace, patience, kindness, goodness, faithfulness, gentleness, and self-control (this comes from Galatians 5:22–23; these virtues are called the "fruit of the Spirit")

- Other qualities: mercy, courage, gratitude, dedication or commitment, strength beyond that of any normal person; super intelligence, leadership

Check your answers against ours at the end of the chapter. You might have different ones. If so, that's okay too!

1. Samson (Judges 16 in the Bible) and Hercules (Greek and Roman mythology)

2. Lucy (*LWW*) and Dorothy (*The Wonderful Wizard of Oz*)

3. Frodo (*Lord of the Rings*) and David (1 Samuel 21–27)

4. Bilbo (*The Hobbit*) and Peter (*LWW*)

5. Mary Lennox (*The Secret Garden* by Frances Hodgson Burnett) and Edmund (*LWW*)

6. Curdie (*The Princess and the Goblin* and *The Princess and Curdie*) and Peter (*LWW*)

7. Princess Irene (*The Princess and the Goblin*) and Lucy

8. Pocahontas and Mulan (from the Disney movies of the same names)

TA-DUH!

𝔐ice on a 𝔐ission

The helpful mice that chewed Aslan's ropes in chapter 15 of *LWW* aren't the only helpful mice in books or movies. Did you know that

- Dressmaking mice in the Disney movie *Cinderella* helped Cinderella make a dress before her fairy godmother showed up?

- Despereaux Tilling, a tiny heroic mouse, saves the day in *The Tale of Despereaux* by Kate DiCamillo (the 2004 Newbery Award winner)?

- Field mice rescued the Cowardly Lion from the deadly poppies in *The Wonderful Wizard of Oz*?

- Two mice (Bernard and Bianca) go on rescue missions in the *Rescuers* movies produced by Disney (*The Rescuers; The Rescuers Down Under*), which are based on the book series by Margery Sharp?

𝔄ll 𝔄bout 𝔖usan

AGE: Around eleven

NICKNAME(S): Su

QUALITIES: Edmund accuses of her trying to sound like their mother; but she's practical and sensible. She is fearful about

Narnia at first. Some other qualities: polite (compliments the Beavers about their dam); helpful; the one who asks whether Aslan is "safe"; gentle; a peacemaker; the only one besides Lucy brave enough to follow Aslan when he surrenders himself to the witch; later becomes "a tall and gracious woman" with extremely long black hair.

CLAIM TO FAME: Does not believe Lucy about Narnia until she goes there herself

LIKES/LOVES: Thinks the Professor is "an old dear"; likes exploring old houses

DISLIKES: When Edmund teases Lucy

GIFT FROM FATHER CHRISTMAS: Bow, quiver of arrows, and an ivory horn

NARNIA TITLE(S): Queen Susan; Susan the Gentle; Daughter of Eve

ANSWERS TO THE HERO(INE) QUIZ

1. Samson and Hercules had amazing strength.

2. Lucy and Dorothy were kind and helpful. They also had enough courage to enter a strange land and help others.

3. Frodo and David had perseverance during the pursuit of a relentless enemy (Sauron pursued Frodo, while Saul, the King of Israel, continually tried to kill David).

4. Bilbo and Peter had the courage to face Smaug and Maugrim respectively.

5. Mary and Edmund start their stories off as unpleasant people. But the changes in their lives caused them to be grateful, which led them to change at the end. So gratitude helped them.

6. Curdie and Peter showed leadership and commitment to their causes.

7. Irene and Lucy showed courage when others didn't believe them. Curdie didn't believe that Irene's great-great-great etc. grandmother existed, because he couldn't see her like Irene could. Lucy's siblings didn't believe her about Narnia.

8. Pocahontas and Mulan showed courage. Both had to go against the ways of their people in order to save the lives of others.

CHAPTER SIXTEEN

A Fight to the Finish

The Great War

What's the bravest thing you've ever done? Complimenting your sister on her outfit even though you think it's ugly? Admitting you were wrong? Facing down a bully? Okay. Those are pretty brave. But you have to admit that fighting in a war is a pretty brave thing to do, too.

If you read about the big battle in chapter 16 of *LWW*, perhaps like us you wondered whether or not Peter was scared or whether Edmund wanted to run away, instead of running into battle.

As we read of Peter's first battle and the big one in chapter 16 (Aslan's army versus the witch's army of evil fairy-tale creatures), we couldn't help thinking about C. S. Lewis. Oh, not because he wrote *LWW*. He could write about war because he participated in one—a war that also reminds us of the one in *LWW*.

Like a lot of young men at the time, Lewis volunteered to fight in the Great War—World War I—soon after being accepted into Oxford University. In fact, he went to Oxford knowing that he would soon have to go off to fight in the war. (If he attended a school in Ireland, he would have avoided the draft.)

Why Go to War?

Now, you might wonder what that war was all about and how C. S. Lewis became involved in it. We'll try to tell you as quickly as we can.[1] (You didn't know this book doubles as a history book did you? See.) It involved a number of nations. (Guess that's why it was called the Great War, or World War I.) Germany, Turkey, and Austria-Hungary (the Central Powers) were on one side. The other side (the Allies) included Great Britain, France, the United States (starting in 1917), Italy, Japan, and Russia. This is the war that eventually led to World War II. (Even wars have sequels, sadly.)

Because Franz Ferdinand, the Archduke of Austria-Hungary (yes, they used to be a dual monarchy), and his wife were assassinated by a secret Serbian group in June 28, 1914, Austria-Hungary demanded justice. Later in 1914 they declared war on Serbia and sent troops to the Balkans. The Germans, allies of Austria-Hungary, became involved to keep the Russians from becoming involved. But the Russians, who had a treaty (an agreement of peace) with Serbia, gathered their troops anyway.

The Germans told France not to get involved. (France and Russia also had a peace treaty.) But the French decided to get *their* troops ready. So, Germany declared war against France!

When the Germans invaded Belgium, Great Britain got involved, having promised France to help protect Belgium. Great Britain declared war against Germany and later Austria-Hungary.

Japan, which had an agreement with Great Britain, declared war against Germany. Austria-Hungary then declared war against Japan.

The United States became involved later, mainly because of Germany.

[1] A great Web site on the war is http://www.firstworldwar.com/origins/causes.htm (You know the drill. Check with parents first.)

Jack-in-the-Box

So, into this whole mess stepped C. S. Lewis and about a million other British soldiers (including Warren Lewis, who was a career officer). C. S. Lewis's tour of duty happened toward the end of the war. But he couldn't know that the war would end a year later.

During cadet training, he became friends with Paddy Moore. Back in chapter 1, we told you that he promised to look after Paddy's mother and sister if anything happened to Paddy during the war.

After his period as a cadet in 1917, Lewis became a second lieutenant in the Somerset Light Infantry. He was just nineteen when he was ordered to the front lines in France. (In fact, he arrived there on his birthday. What a birthday present. We're sure he would've preferred a nice card instead.) There he fought in trenches—those deep ditches soldiers used for cover. It was like being in a dirt box. The conditions were awful.

Lewis didn't escape sickness or injury. After catching what was known as trench fever (pyrexia), he was sent to a hospital for three weeks (which gave him time to read). Later, during the Battle of Arras (a city in northern France) in April 1918, a British shell wounded him. His friend Paddy was declared missing.

In his autobiography, *Surprised by Joy,* Lewis was reluctant to say much about the war or his experiences during it. We do know that he was demobilized (discharged from active service) in January 1919 and returned to Oxford after a long recovery from his wounds. At this point he found out that Paddy was dead. He made good on his promise to care for Paddy's family.

The Final Showdown

So, now you see why C. S. Lewis could write about war. He knew what fighting in a war against an enemy was like. But the battle he describes in chapter 16 of *LWW* has another source of inspiration. Aslan's battle with and defeat of the White Witch, which comes during the big battle in *LWW,* is like the future battle that the Bible says will take place between God's army and Satan's (Revelation 16:16; 19:11–21; 20:1–2). This ultimate battle between good and evil will be fought at a place known as Armageddon. (Yeah, like the title of the old Bruce Willis movie from 1998.)

Many adventure stories have a big battle scene between the forces of good and the forces of evil that mirror this ultimate battle. In westerns, this is usually the final shootout between the hero and the villain(s). In fantasy stories, the final showdown comes when the hero or heroine tries to complete his or her quest. The defeat of the main villain is usually the most satisfying part of a story.

Some battles in fairy tales include

- *The Princess and the Goblin*—The king, Curdie, and Irene versus the goblins

- *The Princess and Curdie*—Evil servants versus Curdie and his army of mutant animals

- *Lord of the Rings: Return of the King*—a number of battles take place against Sauron and his evil forces

- *St. George and the Dragon*—As we mentioned in chapter 12, this is the ultimate battle between a human and a dragon.

This battle also mirrors the one between Jesus and Satan (who is known as "the dragon" in the book of Revelation in the Bible)

- *Sir Gawain and the Green Knight*—Sir Gawain, one of King Arthur's knights, has to fight the famed Green Knight—a man who seems impossible to beat.

- *Beowulf*—A hero of the Geats (not "Greats"; Geats), with the strength of thirty men, battles not one man-eating monster, but two that terrorized the Danes. (C. S. Lewis really liked this story.)

Ding-Dong, the Witch Is Dead

As you know, the White Witch finally comes to the end of the road in chapter 16 of *LWW*. Speaking of witches, there are other fairy tales that involve the end of a witch in some way.

- Dorothy melts the Wicked Witch of the West with a bucket of water in *The Wonderful Wizard of Oz*.

- In *Sleeping Beauty* (the Disney version), the prince defeats the evil fairy after she changes into a dragon.

- In *Snow White* (Disney version), after the Seven Dwarfs run after the evil, black magic–using queen, she winds up falling off a cliff while trying to crush the dwarfs with a rock. (Nasty)

- In "Hansel and Gretel," the witch who tried to cook the kids winds up in the oven herself.

The Breath of Life

The fact that Aslan breathes on the statues and restores them to life is like the power of God as described in the Bible in an Old Testament book called Ezekiel (toward the end, but not at the very end; it's next to the book of Daniel). One story especially reminded us of that, even though the situation isn't exactly the same. A prophet named Ezekiel had a sort of dream where he talked with God. Ezekiel stood in front of a valley filled with bones. God told him he could make the bones live just by breathing on them. But first, Ezekiel had to preach to the bones!

So, he did. And God breathed on the bones, which suddenly came to life—not as skeletons, but as people of flesh and blood.

Another story that talks about breath and life is the Creation story in the Bible. That's in Genesis (the first book of the Bible). When Adam was created, he wasn't yet alive. God "breathed into his nostrils the breath of life, and the man became a living being" (Genesis 2:7, *New American Standard Bible*).

TA-DUH!

Nursery Rhymes

Aslan's words in chapter 16 of *LWW* ("Up stairs and down stairs and in my lady's chamber!") come from the nursery rhyme "Goosey, Goosey, Gander." Perhaps you know it?

Goosey, goosey, gander,
Whither [in some cases, Where] shall I wander?
Upstairs and downstairs,
And in my lady's chamber.

> There I met an old man
> Who wouldn't say his prayers!
> I took him by the left leg
> And threw him down the stairs.

Castles in the UK[2]

In chapter 16 of *LWW*, the Pevensies fight for the privilege they achieve in chapter 17, to be crowned kings and queens of Narnia at Cair Paravel. Peter was given a glimpse of this amazing castle in chapter 12.

Many people think of castles when they think of the United Kingdom (England, Scotland, Wales, Northern Ireland). There are many stone castles throughout the UK—thousands, in fact. Castles got their start in England thanks to William the Conqueror after his troops conquered England in 1066 during the Battle of Hastings (see chapter 14).

When he became King of England (which could happen if you conquer a land), William had castles built not only in England but also in Scotland and Wales. These castles were called *motte and bailey* castles. The *motte* is the hill on which the castle is built. A *bailey* is a courtyard surrounded by castle walls.

Now, you might wonder about some of the other parts of a castle and what they're called. Let's start with the outer wall. Every castle has one. This is known as the *curtain wall*. These walls are really thick—sometimes 20 feet thick.

Another feature of a castle that you've probably noticed are the towers. Towers used to be square for a while until round towers

---

[2] A really cool Web site on castles in Great Britain is http://www.castles-of-britain.com. (Parents, check.)

were discovered to be more stable in a battle situation. (The witch's house has towers with pointed spires. Cair Paravel also has towers.)

Some curtain walls have gatehouses on them, through which can be dropped the *portcullis*. What's a portcullis? An iron gate. (If you saw *Return of the King*, you saw a portcullis in action.)

Some castles have moats in front of them. These are water-filled ditches.

Many castles were entered by the drawbridge—the wooden structure that, when lowered over the moat, formed a bridge to cross over.

SOME CASTLES IN THE UNITED KINGDOM

- Berkeley—This castle was finished in 1153 by Lord Maurice de Berkeley and stands near the Severn River on the border between England and Wales

- Caister—If you're in Norfolk, be sure to look for this castle, which was built in 1432

- Caerleon—A motte and bailey castle, built in 1085 in South Wales. There is a legend that Caerleon was actually the site of King Arthur's palace

- Chepstow—One of the oldest castles in the land, built in 1067, in southeast Wales

- Hever Castle—The childhood home of Anne Boleyn, second wife of Henry VIII and mother of Queen Elizabeth I. Located in Kent, in southern England, part of the castle was built in 1270

- Monmouth—This ancient castle located in Monmouthshire in South Wales was begun in 1068.

- Penhow—Another Welsh castle; this one possibly built by 1129

- Raglan—William ap Thomas, who was knighted by Henry VI, built this castle during the fifteenth century; it is located in Gwent (southeast Wales).

- Thornbury—Another "young" castle, built in 1510 by the third Duke of Buckingham, in south Gloucestershire; it is now a luxury hotel.

- Windsor—This is the house of Queen Elizabeth II and is considered one of the seven wonders of Britain. It is located in Berkshire and was built by William the Conqueror, starting in 1066. According to the official Windsor Castle Web site (http://www.windsor.gov.uk), it is "the largest inhabited castle in the world." Pretty groovy.

All about Giant Rumblebuffin

WHERE WE FIRST MEET HIM: Chapter 16 of *LWW*

OTHER NAMES: Mr. Rumblebuffin (Lucy calls him that)

QUALITIES: He is from a family of good giants (the Buffins)—a rarity in Narnia. Alas, he lacks cleverness.

CLAIM TO FAME: He helps Aslan by breaking the gates and towers of the witch's house.

MISTAKES: Once, he picked up Lucy and almost used her for a handkerchief.

LIKES/LOVES: He loves serving Aslan.

DISLIKES: The White Witch

TITLES HE USES FOR ASLAN: Your honor

CHAPTER SEVENTEEN

All's Well That Ends Well

And They Lived Happily Ever After

How do you feel

- At the end of a tough race?

- At the end of school and the start of summer vacation?

- At the end of a tough project?

- After graduation?

- When you finally get through the last level of a next-to-impossible-to-beat video game?

- When you finally feel better after a long illness?

If you're like us, you feel like celebrating. (Well, you feel like sleeping first, then celebrating.)

That's what happens in chapter 17 of *LWW*. A long hard battle has been fought and won. Those who were hurt are healed. The time has come for a coronation—what the eucastrastrophe of chapter 15 made possible.

Most fairy tales end with some form of "and they lived happily ever after" (or, in some cases, they live with the promise of a new beginning), and *LWW* is no different. A happy event usually leads up to this conclusion. In *LWW,* the Pevensies' coronation is that happy event. But other stories end with a wedding, treasure found and brought back, graduations, a parent's return home, or family love restored. These are the events that bring a fairy tale to a satisfying conclusion.

Mia accepts her role as princess of Genovia (*Princess Diaries*). Cinderella marries the prince. Jim Hawkins returns home with treasure in *Treasure Island.* In *Return of the King* (book and movie), after a long tough road, we see Aragorn's coronation *and* the promise of a wedding. (Although the book does not end after the coronation and the wedding. But Aragorn's part of the story ends here.)

But in *LWW,* after the coronation and huge feast, there was still one final task to complete. Yes, the Pevensies had to rule for several years. But they also had to return home.

Before we get into that, let's talk about the white stag for a bit.

𝔚hat 𝔄bout the 𝔚hite 𝔖tag?

You probably noticed that Peter, Susan, Edmund, and Lucy hunted the white stag, but never caught it. You know how we said that some creatures pop up in many fairy tales (giants, elves, etc.)? Well, the white stag also pops up in many fairy stories. It's a signal that the person pursuing it is just about to cross over into another world. In a way, the white stag is like the wardrobe—something that leads a person to another world or back to his or her own world.

In a Welsh myth C. S. Lewis would have known called "Pwyll, son of Dyved,"[1] hunting a white stag leads a prince (Pwyll) into a world of trouble. Pwyll is forced to serve Arawn, the lord of a

---

[1] This story is just one of several stories in a collection of Welsh stories called *The Mabinogion.* These stories are old—possibly nearly a thousand years old. Anyway, they are actually from two books: *The Red Book of Hergest* and *The White Book of Rhydderch,* both of which were written hundreds of years *before* that.

fairy-tale realm called Otherworld after Pwyll rudely claims a stag that Arawn hunted.

There's a popular Hungarian myth about two brothers (Hunor and Magar) who followed a white stag into Scythia. They remained there and later became two groups of people: the Huns and Magyars.

That's not all we found out about the white stag. Many Christians view it as a symbol of Christ—just like the unicorn (see chapter 13). In fact, some believe that the white stag *is* a unicorn. (Maybe it is, maybe it isn't. We're not sure.)

The white stag is not to be confused with the golden hind. The search for the golden hind in some fairy stories (like "The Hunting of the Hind," in a fairy-tale collection by Robin McKinley, for instance) drove people insane or to their deaths. So, don't search for one.

Return to Reality

The hunt for the white stag led the Pevensies back through the wardrobe and the reality of their childhood. Not only that, they learned that they couldn't get back to Narnia through the wardrobe again! But someday they would return there.

It's hard to return to reality, once you've been in a fantasy world. But sooner or later, everyone gets a wake-up call. Still, there's no place like home.

Here are some others and how they returned to reality:

- Alice leaves Wonderland by waking up

- The silver shoes help Dorothy leave Oz and return to Kansas. But she lost them on the way there (Baum's book has silver shoes; the movie has ruby slippers). In the movie of *The Wizard of Oz,* she wakes up and discovered the whole thing was a dream

- In *The Amulet,* when Cyril, Anthea, Robert, and Jane return to the present for the last time, the event they have been hoping for the entire book happens. (If we told you what that was, you wouldn't read the book.) So, they give away the amulet. And what of the sand fairy? Well, you'll just have to read the book!

- In *The Phantom Tollbooth,* by Norton Juster, Milo leaves the Kingdom of Wisdom (after rescuing the princesses from the Castle in the Air) and drives his car back through the tollbooth in his room

TA-DUH!

A Future Feast

The celebration after the Pevensies' coronation reminded us of a story in the Bible. John, one of the twelve disciples of Jesus, talked about a future feast prepared by God prepared for people in heaven (Revelation 19:7–10). For John (and C. S. Lewis) this is the ultimate happy ending.

Young Rulers

The Pevensies were crowned kings and queens at a young age. Other rulers in stories and in real life gained their thrones at a young age, too. Although some ruled longer than the Pevensies ruled Narnia, others didn't.

- Joash, a ruler mentioned in the Bible, became King of Judah when he was seven (2 Kings 11:21) around 835 B.C. and ruled for forty years.

- Young "Wart" (Arthur), after pulling a sword from an anvil, became King of England. There are so many legends of King Arthur that the length of his reign is questionable. In many stories, he reigned until he reached old age.

- Another kid, Manasseh, was twelve when *he* became King of Judah in 697 B.C. (2 Kings 21:21); he reigned for fifty-five years.

- Clovis I became King of Gaul (later northern France and Belgium) in the fifth century, when he was about fifteen, and ruled for about thirty years.

- Margaret, the Maid of Norway, became Queen of Scotland in 1286 when she was three years old; her reign lasted four years.

- Edward V was twelve when the crown of England was passed on to him; his reign lasted about two months, unfortunately.

- Henry P'u-I became Emperor of China in 1908 at the age of three; his reign lasted three years.

- Tutankhamen, otherwise known as King Tut, reigned over Egypt for about ten years, c. 1370–52 B.C. Since he died when he was about eighteen, he was probably seven or eight when he became king.

- Cleopatra was about eighteen when she became Queen of Egypt (in 51 B.C.). She reigned for over twenty years with other people (like her brothers and son, all of whom were named Ptolemy).

- Francis II (not to be confused with Emperor Francis II of Austria) became King of France in 1559 when he was about fifteen. His reign lasted a year.

Let's Play Jeopardy!

All good things must come to an end, and that includes this book. As we wrap things up, how about a final quiz for starters? Yeah, we thought you'd go for that. Ever play *Jeopardy!*? The answers are in the form of a question. If we were to give this answer: "The lion leader of Narnia," you would respond, "Who is Aslan?" You could be another Ken Jennings! (Remember him—the guy who won seventy-four games of *Jeopardy!*)

CATEGORIES:

1. Characters in *LWW*

2. Location, Location, Location

3. The Ways Things Work

4. Prized Possessions

5. C. S. Lewis Facts Covered in This Book

1. **CHARACTERS IN LWW**

   A. A big gray animal Peter thought was an Alsatian
   B. Their tiny teeth released Aslan from his ropes.
   C. This individual was a "giant" help to Aslan in breaking the witch's gate.
   D. A small sidekick of the White Witch
   E. This half Jinn, half Giantess made a lethal combination.

2. **LOCATION, LOCATION, LOCATION**

   A. In a plain between two hills
   B. The place where four thrones waited for the Pevensies
   C. This place needed a new sluice gate.
   D. The place where Aslan died
   E. This handy hiding place helped out in a pinch.

3. **THE WAY THINGS WORK**

   A. On a fishing trip, this was used to catch a trout.
   B. What Lucy had that wounded people needed
   C. The "horsepower" behind the sledge
   D. According to Aslan, this settles the debt of Edmund's wrong
   E. Lucy took this way to another world.

4. **PRIZED POSSESSIONS**

   A. The one thing Mrs. Beaver couldn't leave behind
   B. Gifts from Father Christmas to Susan
   C. What Edmund craved more than anything
   D. A token from Lucy that showed friendship
   E. The Professor had a lot of rare ones, and Mr. Tumnus did, too.

5. C. S. LEWIS FACTS COVERED IN THIS BOOK

  A. It's divided between logic and imagination
  B. You have two, but C. S. Lewis only had one.
  C. This teacher, who taught Lewis logic, has a nickname like a joke.
  D. A favorite author of Lewis who wrote about five children
  E. This friend liked *LWW*

Oscar Time

Every year, the Academy of Motion Picture Arts and Sciences gets together to honor the movies that have entertained us the previous year. Now that we've come to the end of *LWW*, we thought of the Oscars we would give to the characters of Narnia for their great performances if the Academy would allow us to do so. (Maybe our awards should be called the "Aslans" or "Beavers," in honor of the hardworking king and the delightful Mr. and Mrs. Beaver.) Oh, we'd have to change a few of the categories. But we'd probably come up with a list like the following. How would your list compare with ours? What awards would you add, or take away?

MOST HEROIC NARNIANS The nominees are

  • Aslan

  • Mr. Tumnus (who refused to do the witch's bidding and wound up a statute because of it)

  • The mice who nibbled the cords binding Aslan

  • The animals sent to rescue Edmund from the witch

  • The Beavers

And the winner is . . . Aslan by a landslide!

WORST VILLAIN(S) The nominees are

- The White Witch
- Maugrim
- The Dwarf
- The other wolf (Maugrim's sidekick)
- The witch's army

And the winner is . . . who else but the White Witch?

BEST SUPPORTING CREATURE The nominees are

- The Beavers
- Rumblebuffin
- The sheepdog in chapter 16 who helped Aslan round up everyone
- The two leopards in chapter 12 who were Aslan's servants
- The eager lion in chapter 16 who was happy to be identified with Aslan

And the winner is . . . actually *two* creatures—the Beavers

BEST SUPPORTING HUMAN The nominees are

- Peter
- Susan

- Lucy

- Edmund (for helping in the battle against the White Witch)

- Professor Kirke (for believing in Lucy, even when Peter and Susan didn't)

And the winner is . . . who else but Lucy? Sure, Peter and Edmund (eventually) heroically fought in the battle. But Lucy is the one who found Narnia in the first place! And she's the one who encouraged her brothers and sister to help Mr. Tumnus. She gets props for that.

BEST ART DIRECTION In a movie, this award would go to the people who established the look of a film (the sets). Since no sets were used, we have to give an award to anyone who decorated in any fashion in the book. The nominees are

- The Beavers for their work on their cozy home

- Mr. Tumnus for his cozy cave

- Aslan for creating Narnia

- Professor Kirke and Mrs. Macready for a home worthy of tourists

- The animals in chapter 11 ("Aslan Is Nearer") for their Christmas decorations.

And the winner is . . . Aslan, of course!

WORST ART DIRECTION If we have an award for best art direction, we have to have a worst one as well. The nominees are

- The White Witch for using the creatures she turned into statues in her decorating (chapter 9)

- Edmund with his plans to renovate Narnia (chapter 9)

- Edmund for scribbling a mustache on the statute of the lion (chapter 9)

And the winner is . . . It's a tie: the White Witch and Edmund for scribbling a mustache on the statue of the lion.

BEST PERSONAL STYLE The nominees are

- Mr. Tumnus with his red scraf, umbrella, and tail tastefully draped over one arm

- Mrs. Beaver with her eyeglasses and snow boots

- The birch-girls in silver, the beech-girls in transparent green, the larch-girls in bright green

And the winner is . . . Mr. Tumnus. We can't resist a red scarf.

BEST SOUND Even though you can't "hear" sound in a book, C. S. Lewis described certain sounds. The nominees are

- Aslan's roar

- Aslan's purr

- Susan's horn ("like a bugle, but richer," according to Lewis)

And the winner is . . . Aslan's roar.

JEOPARDY! QUIZ ANSWERS

1. Characters in *LWW*
   A. What is a description of Maugrim? Or, Who is Maugrim? ("Peter's First Battle," chapter 12 of *LWW*)

B. Who are the mice? ("Deeper Magic from *Before* the Dawn of Time," chapter 15)

C. Who is Rumblebuffin? ("What Happened About the Statues," chapter 16)

D. Who is the dwarf? ("Turkish Delight," chapter 4; "In the Witch's House," chapter 9)

E. Who is the White Witch? ("What Happened After Dinner," chapter 8; "In the Witch's House," chapter 9)

2. Location, Location, Location

A. What is the location of the witch's house? Or, Where is the witch's house? ("Turkish Delight," chapter 4; "In the Witch's House," chapter 9)

B. What is Cair Paravel? ("What Happened After Dinner," chapter 8)

C. What is the Beavers' dam? ("The Spell Begins to Break," chapter 10)

D. What is the Stone Table? ("The Triumph of the Witch," chapter 14)

E. What is a cave (the Beavers' hiding place)? ("The Spell Begins to Break," chapter 10)

3. The Ways Things Work

A. What is Mr. Beaver's paw? ("A Day with the Beavers," chapter 7)

B. What is a cordial? ("The Spell Begins to Break," chapter 10; "The Hunting of the White Stag," chapter 18)

C. What are reindeer? ("Edmund and the Wardrobe," chapter 3)

D. What is Aslan's death. Or, the death of an innocent, willing victim ("Deeper Magic from *Before* the Dawn of Time," chapter 15)

E. What is the wardrobe? ("Lucy Looks into a Wardrobe," chapter 1; "Back on This side of the Door," chapter 5)

4. Prized Possessions
   A. What is Mrs. Beaver's sewing machine? ("The Spell Begins to Break," chapter 10)
   B. What are a bow, a quiver of arrows, and an ivory horn? ("The Spell Begins to Break," chapter 10)
   C. What is Turkish Delight? ("Turkish Delight," chapter 4)
   D. What is Lucy's handkerchief? ("A Day with the Beavers," chapter 7)
   E. What are books? ("What Lucy Found There," chapter 3; "Back on This Side of the Door," chapter 5)

5. C. S. Lewis Facts Covered in This Book
   A. What is C. S. Lewis's brain? (chapter 5a of this book)
   B. What are joints in each thumb? (Introduction of this book)
   C. Who is the Great Knock? (Get it? Knock-knock joke?) (chapter 5a of this book)
   D. Who is E. Nesbit? (Introduction and chapter 5b of this book)
   E. Who is Roger Lancelyn Green? (chapter 5b of this book)

Epilogue: The Last Word

The Show Must Go On

Feeling a sense of Narnia withdrawal now that you've finished *The Lion, the Witch and the Wardrobe*? We understand. But you don't have to suffer! If you're ready to take a trip to Narnia again, you have six more chances to do so, starting with

THE MAGICIAN'S NEPHEW (PUBLISHED IN 1955) Although this book was written after *LWW*, the action in the story comes first. It is a prequel—a book that comes before the first book in a series. C. S. Lewis thought that his readers might wonder how Narnia came to be. So, he wrote a whole book that explains how!

In chapter 5a, we told you that the Professor of *LWW* is the star of this book. We weren't kidding. But this story happened when he was a kid. He had quite an adventure, thanks to his evil uncle Andrew. But at least he has a friend named Polly to go along with him.

We would tell you more, but we wouldn't want to spoil your appetite for the book, now would we?

THE HORSE AND HIS BOY (PUBLISHED IN 1954) This is actually the fourth book in the series by C. S. Lewis. But the story takes place during Peter, Susan, Lucy, and Edmund's reigning years as kings and queens of Narnia (see chapter 17 of *LWW*). That era was known as the Golden Age of Narnia. So, chronologically, *The Horse and His Boy* follows *LWW*. (Actually, if fits into the time period covered in chapter 17, right before the Pevensies return to the Professor's house.)

In this story, we meet a boy named Shasta, who discovers a talking horse: Bree. When Shasta runs away from the only home he's ever known, he discovers more adventure than he bargained for. Along the way he meets Aravis, a Tarkheena.

PRINCE CASPIAN (PUBLISHED IN 1951) C. S. Lewis wrote this book right after *LWW*. But it comes fourth in the series now. Although only a year in the Pevensies' lives has passed since the action in *LWW*, one thousand years have passed in Narnia. (How time flies when you're having fun.) The Pevensies meet Prince Caspian, a thirteen-year-old whose evil uncle, Miraz (there seem to be a lot of evil uncles around), has taken over the throne.

This marks the last adventure Peter and Susan will take in Narnia.

THE VOYAGE OF THE DAWN TREADER (PUBLISHED IN 1952) Only Edmund and Lucy make the journey to Narnia this time. With them comes their annoying cousin, Eustace Scrubb, who runs into trouble like Edmund did in *LWW*. (Problems make a story interesting.)

Edmund and Lucy are reunited with Caspian, who is now sixteen and on an important voyage to the ends of the earth.

This is the last adventure Edmund and Lucy will take in Narnia. (But it doesn't have to be your last.)

THE SILVER CHAIR (PUBLISHED IN 1953) This is a favorite of ours, especially since it introduces Puddleglum the Marsh-wiggle. Eustace returns to Narnia with a girl from school: Jill Poole. Their mission from Aslan is to find the lost Prince Rilian, son of the now aged Caspian. Unfortunately, Rilian is a prisoner of the Green Witch (Narnia seems to have colorful witches). Will they accept it? Will Aslan appear? You'll find out if you read this book.

THE LAST BATTLE (PUBLISHED IN 1956) In this book, Aslan has been away from Narnia for a long time. Shift, a scheming ape, dresses Puzzle, a donkey (who isn't the sharpest tool in the shed), in a lion skin to fool everyone into believing that Aslan has returned. But when the real Aslan does return, the battle begins.

Jill and Eustace return once more, along with a more than surprised Peter, Lucy, and Edmund. Jill and Eustace are sent to help King Tirian, the last King of Narnia, and Jewel, his faithful unicorn in the last battle for Narnia.

The Last Battle won C. S. Lewis the Carnegie medal in 1956. This award is given yearly (since 1936) for the most outstanding children's book published in the United Kingdom. It was named after Andrew Carnegie, a Scottish philanthropist. (The Newbery Award is given in America each year for the most outstanding children's book.)

Study Guide: A Book Worth Discussing

The following is a collection of questions pertaining to *LWW*. The questions are laid out by chapter. They can be used as a personal study guide or in a group setting. The intention is to help you think about the book in more depth. Some questions are serious and some are more fun. Groups can use the questions to help with discussions and/or help organize their meetings. Enjoy!

CHAPTER 1

1. During World War II, many children—like the Pevensies—were shipped off to the country to be safer. How would you have felt if you were sent to the country during war?

2. Big, old houses are definitely great for exploration. Share an exploration experience that you have had.

3. When Lucy finds a land full of snow called Narnia, it is quite a surprise. After all, she was just hiding in a wardrobe. A wardrobe is what some people use for closets. What is the strangest thing you have ever found in your closet or what is the strangest thing in your closet right now?

CHAPTER 2

1. Mr. Tumnus, the faun, was going to kidnap Lucy. He decides against handing Lucy over to the White Witch and admits his wrongdoing. The amazing healing power of forgiveness makes it possible for Lucy and Mr. Tumnus to become friends. What qualities do you think are important in a friend?

2. Having afternoon tea is a tradition in both Narnia and Great Britain. Do you and your family have tea together? If so, what is special about teatime for you?

3. Why do you think Mr. Tumnus thinks paying better attention in geography, as a young faun, would have helped him as an adult? Do you think geography is important? Why or why not?

CHAPTER 3

1. Do you think you would have believed Lucy about the magic wardrobe? Why or why not?

2. Edmund's first reaction to Narnia was one of dislike. How do you think his negative thoughts about the place beyond the wardrobe influenced his choices later on in the story?

3. The Queen of Narnia makes a grand entrance on a sledge in this chapter. What would you have said to the strange woman if you were in Edmund's place?

CHAPTER 4

1. Lewis describes the hot drink the witch gave Edmund as "very sweet and foamy and creamy, and it warmed him

right down to his toes." What do you think the beverage was? What warm beverage would you have preferred?

2. It was clear to Edmund what treat he wanted most when asked what he wanted to eat by the White Witch. Would you have accepted the queen's offer of a treat? If so, what would you have asked for?

3. Have you ever tried Turkish Delight? If so, describe what it looked like and whether or not you liked it (see the results of the Turkish Delight survey in chapter 4)

4. Edmund wanted Turkish Delight so badly that he was willing to do whatever it took to taste it again. Have you ever wanted something so much that it made you hurt inside? This type of desire can cause you more pain than good. How can you keep the desire to have more things from not controlling you and keep your thoughts on what is really important?

5. Edmund was intrigued by the idea of becoming a prince. Do you think you would enjoy being royalty? Do you think you would be a good ruler? (Take the quiz "Quest to Rule" in chapter 4)

CHAPTER 5

1. When Edmund proclaimed to Peter and Susan that Lucy's story was false, why were they upset at him instead of Lucy? Explain.

2. Professor Kirke gave Peter and Susan three logical choices about Lucy's strange story. "Either your sister is telling lies, or she is mad, or she is telling the truth," said the Professor in chapter 5. Logically, what conclusion

would you have come to if you were Peter or Susan? Discuss.

3. The Pevensie children were starting to enjoy playing and exploring in the Professor's very large house. What would you have liked about living in the Professor's house in the country? What would you not like?

CHAPTER 6

1. The Pevensie children decide to hide in the wardrobe to be out of the way (Macready's orders). Of course, it is not just an ordinary wardrobe; it is a door to another land, called Narnia. Discuss how you would feel if you discovered a whole new world.

2. The Pevensie children find themselves in a forest of Narnia. What do you think is similar about a Narnian forest and a British forest? What do you think is different?

3. Peter, Susan, Edmund, and Lucy find Mr. Tumnus's home in complete disarray. A note has been left saying that the faun has been arrested. The children must have been very frightened. After all, they were in a world where they did not know the rules. In England, they probably would have called the authorities (police). How do you think their lack of knowledge about Narnia made it more difficult in deciding on what to do?

CHAPTER 7

1. Talking beavers, can you believe it! Narnia is certainly a place that has many new experiences for four British children. By now you have met a faun and two beavers that

can speak. What would be your reaction if an animal in the forest started talking to you? What would you ask Mr. and Mrs. Beaver in Narnia if you had the chance?

2. Chapter 7 introduces Aslan, the King of Narnia. The Pevensie children all feel "something jump" in their insides. Why do you think the children have such a dramatic reaction to the lion's name? Discuss.

3. All the children have different ways of acting as they enter the Beavers' house and are invited for dinner. Peter helps Mr. Beaver catch fish, the girls immediately proceed to help Mrs. Beaver by setting the table, and we are not sure what Edmund is up to (it doesn't say). In what ways can you be helpful when you go over someone's house for dinner?

CHAPTER 8

1. Usually, after a dinner party you find guests doing various things. You may find people laying on the couch patting their tummies and staring off into space. Others may attempt to hold a polite conversation at the table. What do you do after enjoying a nice meal with friends?

2. Have you ever been at a party that suddenly was interrupted by an accident or some bad news or someone missing? Yes, the Beavers and the children all of a sudden realize that Edmund is missing. How would you feel if Edmund were your brother?

3. A prophecy concerning Aslan and Narnia is revealed in chapter 8. What do you think the prophecy means when it says, "Wrong will be right"? Why is it important for Narnia that spring comes again?

4. How did Mr. and Mrs. Beaver know that Edmund was on his way to the White Witch?

CHAPTER 9

1. As Edmund thought about the witch's promises and the taste of Turkish Delight, he became more and more bitter against his siblings. Edmund was also convinced that the other children were ignoring him. Have you ever felt like you were not getting enough attention? How can you prevent yourself from feeling sad and taking it out on others?

2. Edmund had conflicting thoughts about his journey to the witch's house. What thoughts convinced him to continue on his search and not turn back?

3. What is the White Witch's reaction to Edmund's arrival? Do you think Edmund got the welcome he expected?

CHAPTER 10

1. What do you think of Mrs. Beaver's packing? What would you have packed for the journey? Discuss.

2. How is the cave the Beavers and the children sleep in in chapter 10 similar to Mr. Tumnus's cave. How is it different?

3. Why is the arrival of Father Christmas so important? What gifts does Father Christmas give to the Beavers and to the children? Are the presents practical or just for fun? Discuss.

CHAPTER 11

1. Edmund spent time on a sledge (the reindeer-drawn sled) during this chapter. Edmund's ride was unpleasant due to

the company (angry witches can ruin the mood). Have you ever gone on a sled ride in the snow? If so, what did you like or not like about it?

2. The White Witch and Edmund come upon a Christmas party in the wood. This party is full of decorations and food and everyone seems to be having a great time. Do you and your family celebrate Christmas? If so, what Christmas traditions does your family partake in?

3. Narnia is starting to see signs of spring. What do you think the coming of spring signifies in the story? What is your favorite thing about spring?

CHAPTER 12

1. Why do you think the children trembled when they first met Aslan? What qualities make Aslan a true king? What do you think it would be like to meet the Aslan of Narnia?

2. Why do you think Peter took partial blame for Edmund's betrayal? Do you think Peter did anything wrong?

3. Peter experiences his first war shortly after meeting Aslan. Do you think there are reasons to go to war? Why or why not? Why do you think Aslan instructs Peter never to forget to clean his sword after a battle?

CHAPTER 13

1. How does Edmund get rescued in chapter 13? Who do you think sent the rescuers?

2. When Aslan reunites Edmund with his siblings, he instructs them to not talk about the past. Why do you

think Aslan says this? Do you think it was more difficult for Edmund to apologize or for his siblings to forgive him?

3. Do you think it is strange that Aslan would talk with the White Witch alone? What do you think they said to each other?

CHAPTER 14

1. Why do you think Aslan lets Susan and Lucy go with him most of the way to the Stone Table? Discuss.

2. Aslan lets the girls touch his mane; do you think you would have been scared to touch such a majestic beast? Have you ever seen lions in a zoo? What do you think is the most impressive quality of lions?

3. Why does Aslan let the White Witch take his life? Discuss.

CHAPTER 15

1. When Aslan comes back to life, Susan and Lucy think he is a ghost. Do you think you could believe in something so miraculous? How do the girls feel when they realize that their king is truly alive?

2. Aslan has Susan and Lucy ride on his back. Lewis asks readers in chapter 15 to imagine what this would be like. Read Lewis's description of the ride and try to imagine how it felt for Susan and Lucy. Do you think you would enjoy riding on Aslan?

3. After the triumph over death, Aslan tells the girls they are on their way to the witch's house. How do you think Susan and Lucy felt about entering the home of the person who tried to corrupt and kill their brother?

CHAPTER 16

1. How do you think it would feel to be surrounded by statues that you knew were once alive? Aslan then starts bringing the Narnia statues back to life by breathing on them. What is Lucy's reaction upon seeing Mr. Tumnus again?

2. Why were the girls concerned about Aslan bringing the giant back to life? How did Giant Rumblebuffin prove useful?

3. When Aslan and the girls returned, they found another battle taking place. How would you feel to return to a battle after having such a triumph? Discuss.

CHAPTER 17

1. Peter, Susan, Edmund, and Lucy are crowned kings and queens of Narnia. They stay in Narnia for many years to rule. How do they feel about being away from England for so long?

2. How do the Pevensies get back to England? When they return, they are children again and only a few moments of time have passed. How are Narnia time and Earth time different? Discuss.

3. What was your favorite part of *LWW*? Who was your favorite character? Did you learn anything from the story about Narnia; what did you learn?

Your Very Own Narnia Celebration

"Aslan" might show up at your party.
Photo of Sassie by Carrie Pyykkonen

You have completed *LWW*. It's time to celebrate, and we thought it would be fun to have a party. After all, what we have learned about Narnia in *LWW* has been a testament to the festive spirit of the creatures from this land. From tea parties to Christmas celebrations, the people of Narnia know how to get down and party. Even during tough times, like the reign of the White Witch, they still held social gatherings. Lucy enjoyed a cup of tea with Mr. Tumnus and some peaceful music (unfortunately, he was trying to lull her to sleep and kidnap her at the time). The Pevensie children had a dinner party with the Beavers. And do you remember the Christmas celebration that took place when Father Christmas came into town?

Why not plan your own party. Here are some ideas to help you plan your very special Narnia celebration. We've chosen three different themes for a Narnia party. They are only suggestions; pick and choose the ideas you would like to use. Make sure to add your own special touches to your party. Have fun planning and celebrating! Remember to invite your friends from Narnia. These three ideas will get you started . . .

A Mr. Tumnus Tea Party

Invite your guests over for tea. You may want to send invitations or you can invite your guests in person. Offer tea and something small to eat. Tea parties are great for catching up with your friends. Conversations around the table with a nice cup of tea can be very pleasant. You can also plan an activity or two for after tea.

TEACUPS AND SAUCERS If your parents will let you use their teacups and saucers, be very careful. Maybe you can let them know that you are inviting the king of beasts over. If this is not an option, maybe one of these suggestions will help:

- Try finding tea ware at garage sales. This option is not likely to break the bank, and is the least expensive way to get your supplies for the party and start your own collection.

- Have your friends each bring their own cup and saucer. This could be a fun thing to talk about during the tea party. Each guest will have their own story of how they acquired their cup and saucer.

- Pretend. The imagination is a great thing. If you only have old mugs with various designs, or disposable cups that can be used for hot liquids, your party can still be a success. If you use disposable cups, you and your guests can decorate them before having your tea.

TEA OFFERINGS Decide what type of tea you want to serve at your party. English Breakfast would be an appropriate British tea; it comes in both regular and decaffeinated. You may want to offer various types of tea in teabags and provide hot water in a teapot. Remember to have cream or milk and sugar for your guests. Maybe you can get sugar cubes: remember to use your imagination. We have heard that good British children take milk and sugar in their tea.

FOOD Typically at a tea party, the host (that's you) offers the guests some snack-type food. Usually the food is dainty so that the treat can be eaten with the hands with little or no mess. Here are a few food suggestions for your tea party: Turkish Delight, finger sandwiches, cookies (perhaps shortbread), crackers with jam, cupcakes, or some other nice treat that you think your guests would enjoy.

ACTIVITIES After tea you may want to plan an activity or two. Mr. Tumnus played music for his guest; maybe you can provide music for your guests. You could also play a game. One idea would be to have a handkerchief-folding contest in honor of Mr. Tumnus. Provide a handkerchief for each of your guests and give everyone three minutes to fold their handkerchief into something useful or funny. Whoever has the most creative idea after three minutes is the winner. You may want to have a prize for the contest or you may want to have party favors (little gifts for your guests to let them know you appreciate that they came). Here are a few ideas:

Prizes/Party Favors: an umbrella or umbrella stickers, a handkerchief, a copy of *LWW,* tea, a teacup, sugar cubes, or a box of cookies.

A Beaver Family Bash

Plan a party for your family. Make an ordinary dinner at home special by adding a Mr. and Mrs. Beaver flare. You could make place tags (a name sign to indicate where that person should sit) for each of your family members. Decorate the tags with a beaver or a fish drawing. Your parents may agree to make the special beaver food for this special party, but be sure you set the table and clean up. Here are some ideas for a very beaver family bash.

A MENU THAT MR. AND MRS. BEAVER WOULD LOVE Mr. and Mrs. Beaver provide a wonderful meal for the Pevensie children in *LWW*. The meal includes bread and butter, boiled potatoes, pan-fried fish, milk, tea, and marmalade rolls. You may want to substitute some of the food for similar items your own family enjoys; for example, you may want to serve fish sticks instead of pan-fried fish, French fries instead of boiled potatoes, and sticky buns instead of marmalade rolls. During dinner you could take turns telling stories. After dinner, if your family has a fireplace, you may want to enjoy a nice fire while sipping tea or reading out of a favorite book.

A Royal Dinner Party

This is your chance to go all-out. Have your guests come dressed up as if they were going to a ball and/or have crowns for all the guests to wear. Then have your guests each make their royal goblet (cup) for the meal by taking plastic cups and gluing plastic jewels on them with craft glue. Serve your guests a royal meal at a nicely set table. You may want to choose a king and queen for the evening. After your royal meal, have all your guests take the

"Quest to Rule Quiz" in chapter 4 (p. 38). It may be fun to have a prize for the person who gets the highest score or the people who become Aslan's chosen according to the quiz. Here are a few ideas for prizes:

Prizes/Party Favors: a stuffed animal lion, a copy of *LWW*, lion stickers, a crown, candy shaped like jewelry, or any other "royal" prize you can think of.

FOOD FIT FOR A KING Here is a list of possible menu items for your royal dinner: A roast or turkey with gravy; king salmon (for fish lovers); royal punch (mix fruit juice with a lemon-lime flavored soda); baked or mashed potatoes; and cake in the shape of a castle or crowned cupcakes (cupcakes with mini-crowns on them).

Planning Your Party

We hope that this chapter gave you some ideas to help you plan your *LWW* theme party. Remember to have fun with it by adding things you and your family and friends like. Find ways to incorporate your favorite parts of the book into your party. If you love the lamppost in the book, you could draw a lamppost on a cake with frosting or make miniature lampposts with your guests at the party. If Aslan is your favorite character in the book, make sure he finds his way into your party plans. The possibilities are endless. We hope you have fun planning and partying!

About the Authors

JAMES STUART BELL is the owner of Whitestone Communications, a literary development agency. He was Director of Religious Publishing at Doubleday. He has written and compiled over forty books, including the best-selling *Complete Idiot's Guide to the Bible*. He lives in the western suburbs of Chicago.

CARRIE PYYKKONEN has degrees in early childhood education and geography. She became interested in Narnia as a young child and has ever since loved fantasy stories. She lives in Wheaton, Illinois, with her husband, two children, and a cat named Sassie. Her interests range from embarrassing her family while dancing in public to partaking in weekly pizza and movie nights.

LINDA WASHINGTON has written several books for kids, including *Just Plain Mel* and *Gotta Have God* (with Jeanette Dall). She lives in Carol Stream, Illinois, and often mooches meals off the Pyykkonens. Also, she likes having serious discussions with her nephew, Samuel, about Pokémon and other Gameboy Advance games.

When she was a child, she read *The Lion, the Witch and the Wardrobe* in serial form and loved it. Who knew that she would grow up (some would say otherwise) to co-author a book about it?